T0307905

JOHN H. BURDAKIN

JOHN H. BURDAKIN

Railroader

Don L. Hofsommer

Michigan State University Press

East Lansing

∞ The paper used in this publication meets the minimum requirements of ANSI/NISO Z39.48-1992 (R 1997) (Permanence of Paper).

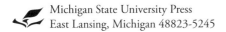 Michigan State University Press
East Lansing, Michigan 48823-5245

Printed and bound in the United States of America.

22 21 20 19 18 17 16   1 2 3 4 5 6 7 8 9 10

LIBRARY OF CONGRESS CONTROL NUMBER: 2015939352
ISBN: 978-1-61186-177-8 (cloth)
ISBN: 978-1-60917-464-4 (ebook: PDF)
ISBN: 978-1-62895-236-0 (ebook: ePub)
ISBN: 978-1-62896-236-9 (ebook: Kindle)

Book design by Scribe Inc. (www.scribenet.com)
Cover design by Erin Kirk New
Cover artwork from the Grand Trunk Corporation/author's collection.

g green press **INITIATIVE** Michigan State University Press is a member of the Green Press Initiative and is committed to developing and encouraging ecologically responsible publishing practices. For more information about the Green Press Initiative and the use of recycled paper in book publishing, please visit www.greenpressinitiative.org.

Visit Michigan State University Press at
www.msupress.org

Contents

Foreword by Dennis J. Gilstad   vii

Preface   ix

Chapter 1. A Contributive and Constructive Life   1

Chapter 2. Firm Foundations   5

Chapter 3. The Standard Railroad of the World   11

Chapter 4. Out of Canada   21

Chapter 5. A Patient Approach   33

Chapter 6. Taking Stock   47

Chapter 7. Jilted   61

Chapter 8. Soldiering On   73

Chapter 9. A Great Ride   93

Notes   99

Index   109

Foreword

Dennis J. Gilstad

I HAVE WORKED AROUND RAILROADS ALL MY LIFE. I LOVE THE INDUSTRY AND ITS people, and none more so than John H. Burdakin, the finest railroad executive I've ever known—and I've known just about all of them. Many of those executives were talented leaders, but none, in my opinion, could match John Burdakin. That judgment is the reason behind this book.

John, in his years with the Pennsylvania Railroad and then as president of the Grand Trunk Railroad, changed the rough, top-down style of railroad management to a style that, while still strong, was professional, respectful, and successful.

I think it's important to share—with students, railroad managers, and general readers—the story of Burdakin's career. By understanding what motivated him and how he motivated others, new generations of railroaders can seek to emulate his example.

In 2008, I donated a million dollars to establish a railway management program at Michigan State University in East Lansing, the most comprehensive training program for railway executives in the nation. This is a time of great change in the railroad industry, and it comes at a time when many of the industry's leaders are retiring, making the need all that much greater for good managers.

Those of us who are railroaders know the work is a calling, with a culture that demands mental toughness, creativity, hard work, and integrity. Managing a railroad requires leadership, problem-solving, and people skills. And it demands profits, but not at the expense of safety.

Not many people are up to that challenge. I know. In 1997, my company, FCM, bought into the Tuscola & Saginaw Bay Railroad, and I became the railway's president and board vice chairman. It was the fourth largest railway in Michigan. I sold my interests in the four-hundred-mile short line in 2006 but, for more than nine years, was a railroad president myself.

Very few railway executives can do what John Burdakin did for the Grand Trunk Western Railroad: Transform a mess into a class act.

Even into his nineties, John's mind was sharp, and he had amazing recall of the years when he was responsible for up to 4,500 Grand Trunk employees. I want to thank him for his hard work on this book and on another book we're doing on his exceptional family and career. I also want to thank railroad historian Don L. Hofsommer and my friend and colleague Gary M. Andrew for their work on this book.

Without John's insights, and the thoughts from those who remember him with as much admiration as I, this book would not have been possible.

Preface

THIS IS A BIOGRAPHY OF JOHN HOWARD BURDAKIN, NOT A CONVENTIONAL BIOGRAphy, but one that focuses on his career as a manager in the railroad industry, stressing his foundational principles—how he came by them, how he applied these values as a manager, and how they were understood by those who worked for him or worked with him.

Burdakin's career was capped off as a senior executive at Grand Trunk Western and then as head of Grand Trunk Corporation. Portions of this work appeared earlier in *Grand Trunk Corporation: Canadian National Railways in the United States, 1971–1992*. (Internal sources cited therein at the time were housed at the GTC office building in Detroit.)

Many persons gave generously of time and resources to bring this project to fruition. Earl C. Fontaine, Gloria R. Combe, Marc Higginbotham, Robert vom Eigen, David J. DeBoer, James Hagen, John W. Barriger, James Krikau, James A. Brewer, Virginia Czarnik, Veronica Cabble, Howard D. Nicholas, Larry Baggerly, Eugene Shepard, Charles Hrdlicka, Phillip R. Larson, Ronald L. Batory, Howard M. Tischler, Mar Sclawy, Art Fettig, George L. Stern, and Annette Mily Duffany gave patiently and generously of memories and insight.

William J. McKnight was especially helpful in any number of respects, including supply of executive speeches and excellent advice about the study—all with cheeriness and willingness to help. The same was true of Gary M. Andrew, who served as liaison throughout. And, as might be expected, John Burdakin provided useful, candid, and detailed comment.

The idea for this biography came from Dennis Gilstad. He is the founder of the feast.

To all of the above, and to Ann E. Anderson, who puts all of this in order, and to any others I might regrettably have overlooked, I am indebted. For errors of fact and for infelicities of style, I alone am responsible.

Chapter 1

A Contributive and Constructive Life

DESIGNED BY ALBERT KAHN AND OPENED TO GREAT FANFARE IN APRIL 1915, THE
Detroit Athletic Club was then and would continue to be the main social club of the community. Located at 241 Madison Avenue and down the street from Detroit's historic Music
Hall, the large, square, seven-story brick structure with high arched windows vaulting upward
from the fourth floor and with ornamentation at the cornices, the "DAC," as it is known
locally, stands boldly if silently as a positive symbol of status, stability, and permanence for
the Motor City.

On the evening of Friday, September 11, 1987, upwards of two hundred persons would
gather in the huge second floor meeting room under the twenty-foot ceiling with giant wooden
beams, to honor John Howard Burdakin on his retirement from Grand Trunk Corporation
and its several component parts. Orchestrated by GTC president Gerald Maas and meticulously planned over time, the event would be singular in elegance. Invited guests included
company directors and senior officers and their wives, business associates, Canadian National
president Ron Lawless, former Canadian National president Robert Bardeen and his wife,
and, of course, Burdakin's wife Jean as well as family members.

A sumptuous meal was followed by the program. Gerald Maas and Ron Lawless offered
remarks—a mix of mild "roast" and heartfelt "toast"—and then John Burdakin took the
microphone.

Burdakin thanked Maas and Lawless in turn. "I have been pleased with the aggressive programs undertaken by Gerry Maas since I left the presidency," he said, and added,
"I believe the transition came at the proper time." Lawless, he noted, was "facing major
problems and challenges in guiding Canadian National through the rough seas of deregulation." But CN was in good hands. Indeed, "Ron has the universal reputation in the U.S.
as Mr. Canadian National and in fact Mr. Railroad of Canada." Then Burdakin pointed to
Robert Bandeen, who had "designed and executed the creation of Grand Trunk Corporation, the independence of the American properties, and the environment for Grand Trunk
Western (GTW) to be a responsive extension of CN and also become self-sufficient." To
be sure, "Bob Bandeen is the one responsible for the success of our three properties." And
it was Bandeen who had brought Burdakin to Grand Trunk in 1971. Not to be forgotten
was Jean—"true wife, partner, confidant, and friend . . . always at my side . . . the foundation for the success that . . . I have achieved or will have achieved in living a contributive
and constructive life."

1

This photograph shows John Burdakin with his beloved wife Jean.

With acknowledgments completed, Burdakin turned a dry eye to an appraisal of his time at Grand Trunk. "In reflection," he began, "the disappointments are small compared to the accomplishments." It seemed a curious start, apparently putting disappointments ahead of accomplishments, but it was pure Burdakin. His would be an unemotional assessment. Yes, of course he was "proud of the record that all of us in this room contributed to make the GTW of today. The company is probably the most respected of the smaller Class I roads in the United States. Our people—Bill Glavin, Jim McNutt, Walter Cramer, and Howard Tischler among them—have served as leaders in their fields. When they ask to be heard, they are allowed to speak and the industry listens." Shippers, too, "now see GTW" as "a skilled organization with respected and competent management. You can be proud that you are a member of this professional and skilled group."

Burdakin recalled that when he arrived on the property in 1971 "the shareholder [Canadian National] was close to the end of providing continued support." True enough. But after a long history of piling up red ink, "GTC and soon after GTW were able to generate a profit and provide our own funds for capital investments in track and rolling stock"—at the same time "improving our responsiveness to our shippers" and "maintaining our obligation to provide a safe, stable work environment." In all of this there was ample reason for pride.

Burdakin likewise took pleasure in recalling acquisition of the strategically placed Detroit, Toledo & Ironton—an acquisition accomplished against great odds favoring much larger applicants. Yes, there were bumps, but "the transition in ownership, the assumption of their employees into GTW, was accomplished with the minimum disruption to operations and to all employees. And when disruption was inevitable, the company handled it in a fair and responsible manner."

Like all other railroad companies at the time, GTC constituent roads struggled to adjust to the realities of the new, mostly deregulated environment. "Deregulation demands tremendous energy, extensive commitment, and new approaches," Burdakin reminded. The GTC roads were small compared to competitive giants nearby that boasted bountiful "market power," but as Burdakin looked to the future, he was extremely optimistic because the GTC holding company and its railroads had in place strong boards of directors and sound management teams—"a solid foundation and heritage."

"There have been disappointments as well as achievements," recalled Burdakin, and "I leave with tasks incomplete and unfulfilled." Here was bittersweet. "The biggest disappointment was our failure to acquire the Milwaukee Road. I am still confident that our plans would have proven ultimately better for shippers, the public, and employees." His second major disappointment derived from his inability to convince the industry to embrace Automatic Car Identification (ACI), an electronic information system designed to locate and identify all of the company's freight cars and trains at a moment's notice—a plan that would have provided the most comprehensive network in the North American railroad industry. These irritating twin burrs would remain forever under Burdakin's saddle.

"And so," John H. Burdakin said in conclusion, "I am pleased that you all are celebrating with Jean and John tonight. I am leaving the daily involvement for the role as a director. I am proud of having been your president; I am proud of the effort you have made to achieve successes. I trust I have been an effective leader, a balanced decision maker, and that I have instilled respect and professionalism to the GT family. I wish you all personal happiness and health. Thank you for giving Jean and I a great trip on the Grand Trunk."[1]

Chapter 2

Firm Foundations

THE YOUNGEST OF THREE CHILDREN IN THE FAMILY OF L. RICHARD BURDAKIN AND Martha Gertrude Burdakin, John Howard Burdakin was born in Milton, Massachusetts, on August 11, 1922. Happy to say, parents L. Richard and Martha would provide young John with a broad and firm foundation of principles and values.[1]

Richard attended a private prep school but had no opportunity for higher education. He was a successful salesman for an important steel boiler manufacturer until the Great Depression, when the company went under—taking the Burdakin family's rosy prospects with it. Father Richard was devastated, financially and emotionally; his career, as it developed, was upside down, a struggle with lots of disappointments. He made ends meet during the 1930s by taking whatever employment offered itself—selling vacuum sweepers, stocking shelves at an A&P grocery store, working on a Work Projects Administration project, and finally signing on as a laborer in a shipyard at Quincy. A coronary problem ended his employment in 1941; he died a decade later. All of this, John Burdakin later would recall, "had a future bearing on my thinking for a career."[2]

Martha was a couple years younger than Richard, "a very strong, solid person." "Mother," John said with emphasis, "was the team leader."[3]

But in all cases it *was* a team. Together they emphasized a doctrine of fairness: "Everybody is a human being and is to be treated as such." They did not "put on airs," and they displayed profound disgust for anybody who "gussied up." The Burdakin children learned from mother and father "not to go around bragging," and every member of the family was obliged to make a "proper contribution." "Everybody has to get an oar in the water and pull, . . . [has to] work hard, . . . [not] lay down on the job . . . [not to] lean on the shovel the better part of the day," to be persistent, to accept responsibility while also "acknowledging generous help from others along the way." "Dad," Burdakin recalled, "did not say much, but when he spoke, you wanted to listen." Further, "Mother and Dad taught me: If I wanted to do it I could get it done. And, if we're going to do it, let's do it well. As Dad put it: Do something you want to do and do it the best you can."[4]

The institutional church was important, especially to Martha Burdakin, less so for Richard, although he certainly believed in and embraced Christian principles. Whether it sprang from theological roots or not, John Burdakin early on concluded that "God planted me on earth . . . to make the world a better place for other people. My mother and father probably planted the 'seed' . . . but I do not recall any discussion with Mother and Dad in this regard."[5]

A very young John Burdakin checks his running gear, an auspicious glimpse into the future.

There were, of course, important outside influences. While Cub Scouts were never of interest—"I could learn more from *Popular Mechanics*"—under Mr. Harding at Quincy's Boy Scout Troop 3, "Here was something I could learn." Eventually Burdakin earned the "Star rank . . . and nine or ten merit badges." This would result in a lifelong support for the Boy Scouts, "a valuable movement for developing young boys."[6]

Parents Richard and Martha put indelible trust in son John and allowed him in many ways to chart his own course. "As long as they knew what I was doing, I was allowed to go and do things that today you wouldn't think of, such as probably at age of nine I was given enough money to get into Boston and a little map to go to George Marsh's store and buy model airplanes . . . I knew where the sporting goods store was and where I might get lunch. Mother would send me off on a Saturday morning and I would come back Saturday afternoon late. And maybe they worried about me. . . . I can remember three of us. I was probably eleven, my friend was eleven, and his cousin was thirteen maybe. We went off to Boston and on to New York and took the night bus and spent two nights in the YMCA in New York. Be unheard of today."[7]

Furthermore, "As long as they knew where I was, they made sure I was exposed to most everything that young people should be exposed to, knowing what's going on in the world." That included "playing sports, all kinds of sports." But it was hardly all fun and games. "Mother insisted that, "since I was going to live there, twenty-five cents of my paper route [delivering the *Quincy Patriot-Ledger*] went to support the house every week." This at once reflected twin profound pillars of the Burdakin household philosophy: the importance of work and the importance of responsibility.[8]

Foundational principles likewise were evident and mirrored in Burdakin's schooling. Certain teachers made particular impact. "Mr. Smoyer was a typical English teacher, looked English, John Bullish with the bald head and a fringe of hair, always wearing a vest, about fifty-five, and rather portly, but a superb teacher and a superb person. I had the fortune of taking English with him for three years. He certainly had an impact on my life, even though I finally achieved a grade B in the last term of my senior year and, in his words, not because I earned it but because I tried hard. So a straight amount of Cs was crowned with a B. There were others, of course. The French teacher and I were not on the same frequency, and I took two years of French, but that was more than enough.

Delivering newspapers reflected twin founding principles—work and responsibility.

But my Latin teacher was a superb human being." Burdakin graduated from North Quincy High School in 1940 (twenty-first in a class of three hundred).[9]

Hard times of the 1930s persisted, and the very limited financial position of the family cast a negative shadow on any prospect for higher education. Nevertheless, "Mother and Father never let any other thought but go to college enter my mind. How to get this done with no funds . . . My original goal was to go to West Point." But Burdakin failed the exam—deficient in ancient history and in physics. Disappointed but undaunted, Burdakin exhibited another foundational principle, perseverance: "Grit your teeth and go after it." An application was made to MIT, and he was accepted for the fall term 1940.[10]

How was he going to pay? MIT promised a scholarship to cover half of costs, there were meager savings, an uncle who ran a book store at Fall River promised to kick in substantial support, and another relative "gave me $25 a month as long as I stayed in school." Student loans also were available, and MIT "was a place to which I could commute, and my parents said that they would keep a roof over my head and keep me fed." In the end: "More of that old philosophy Mother and Dad taught me: If I wanted to do it, I could get it done."[11]

What was he going to study? "Engineering was always in my mind. I liked the outdoors, and that seemed to be outdoor-type work. So engineering was a direction, mainly mathematics, science, and that sort of thing where I was interested." And at MIT he found an excellent professor in J. B. Baboon. John appreciated "the way he explained, the way he conducted himself . . . a really fine gentleman, a good, solid, likeable person."[12]

This, of course, was the time of World War II, and Burdakin would be drawn into it. "In the first two years at MIT you had to take beginning ROTC—primarily a little bit of military marching and a few other things. At the end of two years, if you wanted to, you could apply to go on to senior ROTC, and when you graduated with a degree you also were commissioned as a second lieutenant in the Army Reserve. That provided one with a little bit of money every month as long as you stayed in the program. And it certainly held some interest for me, so I applied for that." The military in 1943 decided it needed newly minted officers in a hurry, "So we were put into the regular army, told to take basic training in lieu of fourth-year ROTC, move into Officer Candidate School. And in my case, I was sent to Fort Belvoir (Corps of Engineers) and got my commission as a second lieutenant in the summer of 1944. Most of my military career, almost all of it, was spent in some sort of training program."[13]

"The first job I had was assistant supervisor at a surveying school run by the Engineer Corps teaching different kinds of military surveying: laying out roads, buildings, mapmaking, that sort of thing. Then I wound up in Louisiana teaching basic training to raw recruits for six months or so. Went from there back to Fort Belvoir, which is in Virginia, where I was put in charge of the heavy equipment facet of the school. I ran power shovels, air compressors, and taught enlisted men how to use the machinery and take care of it." Discharge came in October 1946.[14]

What lessons did the army experience provide? It clearly built personal confidence. "I learned that I could stand in front of people, that they would follow you if you told them what to do and how to do it—if you did this patiently and clearly." And, importantly, "When placed in charge, take charge," and "If you are going to do it, do it right."[15]

Burdakin returned to MIT in the fall of 1946 and graduated in June 1947 with a degree in civil engineering.

Military experience taught Burdakin that "when placed in charge, take charge."

John Howard Burdakin and Jean Campbell Moulton were married on October 2, 1948. They had met the year earlier when John was a senior at MIT and Jean was a senior at Radcliffe and, according to John, "soon realized, formally or informally, that maybe this would be a permanent union." "John and I would have been married earlier," Jean recalled, "but I had promised my parents that if they would agree for me to go to my choice, Radcliffe, rather than their choice for me, Bridgewater Normal School, I would work for one year after graduation. I worked as assistant to the registrar at college—a promise kept."[16]

Theirs clearly was an admirable marriage—they deeply loved each other, and they were at the same time very good friends. The unstated but clearly implied message: Choose your mate well. Jean said of John that "he held me in the palm of his hand with kind words, endless patience, and love." And John truly was devoted to Jean. She was a paragon of patience, smart as a whip, "not a show-off," and for her "life was too short to complain." Her motto: "Bloom where you are planted." Why did this marriage succeed? "We appreciated each other," said John. "We had mutual goals in life; she was the glue that kept us together." Most of all, "We were a team." Teamwork: A hallmark Burdakin value.[17]

John and Jean were married on October 2, 1948. In this photograph, Burdakin's parents are on the left.

Chapter 3

The Standard Railroad of the World

DEGREE IN HAND, MILITARY SERVICE COMPLETED, IT WAS TIME TO FIND APPROPRIATE
employment. The long shadow of the Great Depression and its impact on Burdakin's father—
who had lost what he thought was a safe position when the small company he worked for went
belly-up, suggested that greater security might be found with larger concerns. These included
railroad companies that, during the Depression and then World War II, had not hired or
could not hire managers, and now surely found the need to add talent. The size of the organization and the potential for early advancement drew Burdakin's attention to Pennsylvania
Railroad (PRR)—often referred to as the "standard railroad of the world." A deal was struck.[1]

PRR had an impressive and well-structured training program that was designed to expose
new hands like Burdakin to broad aspects of the railroad enterprise and get them ready for
supervisory positions. On-the-job training began on the engineering side of the railroad at New
York's Penn Station, then to the test department at Altoona, Pennsylvania, and then to work
under track supervisors at Lewistown, Pennsylvania, and Jamesburg, New Jersey. PRR's training program was set up on a two-and-a-half year basis, but after a year Burdakin earned his first
supervisory job on a branch line from Trenton to South Amboy in central New Jersey and then
to a portion of the Panhandle Division main line between Pittsburgh and Columbus, where he
was responsible for track maintenance—including ties, rail, drainage, and appearance.[2]

It was during the time Burdakin was on the Ohio job that he experienced his saddest day
railroading when a regularly scheduled passenger train rear-ended a stalled passenger extra carry-
ing Pennsylvania National Guardsmen at West Lafayette, about twelve miles east of Coshocton,
Ohio. Thirty-two people died in the collision. Burdakin's boss was on vacation at the time, so
it fell to him to deal with the local trainmaster to clear the wreck and open the line. "It was a
huge education for me," Burdakin shook his head in recalling the awful calamity. Danger, he
knew, always lurked around the tracks, but this provided a searing and indelible reminder for
the constant need for safe practice.[3] Other lessons came from more positive experiences. From
John McGee, track supervisor at Coshocton, Burdakin, to be sure, learned more about maintaining track, but also "how to get his own boss motivated"—to get his own superior to come
around to agreeing to and then authorizing worthy improvements that originally he had stood
against. By the same token, McGee had the ability to very clearly articulate his disappointment
of performance by those who reported to him. "John," said McGee in instructing his young
protégé, "you can criticize a man for his performance, but don't criticize him for his personal
characteristics; don't call him stupid or dumb. When you get through, leave him with a bit of

Burdakin's job assignments at PRR included time on some of that company's electrified operation. Enola, Pennsylvania, April 1961. (Chris Burger photograph.)

a smile on his face and a bit of respectability. You can embarrass him and make him feel pretty low, but before you leave him, bring his back up." McGee, Burdakin concluded, had a firm grip on "how to manage people—on how to properly emulate going forward."[4]

Another powerful object lesson came from George Schutz, a trackman at Lewistown, Pennsylvania. He may have had only an eighth grade education, but he was a man who, sitting under an apple tree, gave Burdakin an exacting tutorial on string lining a curve. "It's a rather simple mathematical procedure . . . so simple that MIT didn't bother to teach it, so . . . George taught me how to do that. George was a super human being, had a good family. He had as much brain-power as I did," but his father had been injured in a mine accident, so Schutz never had a chance at education. The lesson? "There are a lot of smart people who do not have a college education." Learn wherever you can and from whomever you can—and give credit for this when credit is due.[5]

In 1958, George Vaughn, General Manager of the Eastern Division, told Burdakin that he wanted him to move from engineering to operations and to accept an introductory position as assistant trainmaster at Louisville, Kentucky. In the next year he was off to Cincinnati, Ohio, in the same position. Cincinnati was a "screwed up terminal . . . the godamnest mess I ever saw." Here Burdakin would win his spurs or not.[6]

Shortly after arriving in Cincinnati, Burdakin sought out Jimmy Gelease, the local union representative. "They tell me that Cincinnati's in a hell of a shape," said Burdakin as each man took the measure of the other. "You and I have a problem here. This terminal is tied up tighter than a bull's ass at fight time, and there's no goddamn reason for it." Burdakin continued, "the way I look at it, between you and me, we've gotta straighten out this terminal, and you know, I'm gonna need your help. You're gonna need my help. We'd be better off not starting with boxing gloves on—why not see if we could get along?"[7]

The test of this arrangement was not long in coming. On a nocturnal tour of one of PRR's Cincinnati properties, Burdakin discovered perhaps a dozen men sitting around a table at a yard office—not switching cars as they were hired to do—with playing cards and money on the table. Burdakin introduced himself as the men hurried to get cards and money off the table and exit the room. "Wait a minute fellows, I'm not through yet. You all have a rubber stamp that you use to put your name on the time sheet. Here's a piece of paper. As it goes around, put your stamp on there. I have a little army experience about playing poker and this looks like a poker game. Anybody got a different opinion?" Silence. "I think you're all qualified on the book of rules. . . . It seems to me that poker is gambling and gambling is against the rules." Silence. "You all know that the book of rules says no gambling just like no drinking. You just don't do it." Silence. "I know what goes on at night around here and it's gonna change. Now that I've got names and employee numbers I'll consider what to do. You all go back to work and do what you're supposed to be doing." They all left into the darkness of night. Not surprisingly Gelease appeared at Burdakin's office early the next morning. "What are you gonna do about it?" Gelease wondered. "Damned if I know," Burdakin replied, "but you come back late this afternoon and I will tell you." They met again hours later. "This has been going on a long time," Burdakin blurted out. "I could fire all of them." Then he calmed. "It did not start on my watch—it wasn't my responsibility at the time when this game started. But now it *is* mine." Gelease fidgeted. Each looked at the other in silence. Then, said Burdakin softly but evenly, "Since it was not my responsibility before I got here, I don't think I'm going to do much about it." Gelease was puzzled. "You're not going to hold an investigation?" Gelease asked incredulously. "No," responded Burdakin, "but if I catch this going on again you be prepared to come in with whomever I catch." Gelease nodded his head in agreement and in relief, got up, headed for the door, turned and said: "Thank you." "Just a minute, Jimmy," replied Burdakin, "got something I want to give you." It was the piece of paper with the stamped names and employee numbers. "If you see these fellows tell them we're gonna live by the rules here. You're responsible for these men as much as I am. You know, you're here to watch their jobs, and I am here to watch what jobs they're doing." Burdakin added, with a twinkle in his eye, "We can get along." Get along they did. Gelease and the men came to respect Burdakin because of his devotion to the book of rules, yes, but much more for his fairness.[8]

Safety, or the lack of safe working practice and habit at Cincinnati, also was an issue of great importance. To partially meet that issue and to promote "no lost time injuries," Burdakin had a four-foot by eight-foot sheet of plywood painted and erected as a "Safety Board" where employees going on duty would be reminded that theirs was a dangerous occupation and that they should watch out for their own welfare by working safely and demanding the same of others.[9]

Life then took an interesting twist. Burdakin was asked if he would take a leave of absence to be in charge of the railroad division of the Panama Canal. The answer was yes, and the entire family moved to the Canal Zone for fourteen months. This was a particularly broadening experience, indeed Burdakin's first opportunity to deal with all facets—engineering, operations, sales, rates, budget, and working with the federal government as well as the Panamanian government. The pay was good, the work was enlightening, life in the Canal Zone was rewarding, and Burdakin and family met many interesting personalities.[10]

The entire family moved to the Canal Zone for fourteen months.

Then it was back to Pennsylvania Railroad in Philadelphia as manager of transportation engineering, an industrial engineering position dealing with aspects such as classification yards, synchronization of trains, and teletype communication. Two projects aimed at saving money and improving operation—a weigh in motion scale at Philadelphia and use of radio on trains in the DelMarva Peninsula—occupied much of Burdakin's time. When they were complete they were sent up to one Park Roeper (vice president of transportation and maintenance)—a man at once bombastic, peevish, touchy, high strung, inflexible, and negative. Roeper threw both proposals back in Burdakin's face, asking, "Anything else?" Totally dismayed and thoroughly demoralized, Burdakin left the office and walked the streets of Philadelphia for several hours debating all the while whether he should quit. "If this is the way the mighty Pennsylvania Railroad is going, maybe it is time to bail out." In fact, Park Roeper and this incident did reflect a downward spiral for the "standard railroad of the world," but with a wife and family at home, quitting for Burdakin did not seem like a responsible option. For that matter quitting was not in the Burdakin DNA. But Park Roeper did provide an object lesson. Here was a person well up PRR's managerial ladder who clearly had the power to drive talent from the organization—if only by his obtuseness, his indifference, and his ugly persona—that had been recruited and brought along in an enlightened and progressive way by the company, talent once lost difficult and maybe impossible to replace. Here indeed was a person who could and did create a climate of inordinate caution, suppressing both initiative and élan, who saw issues solely in black and white, and who was impatient with any other possibility. Burdakin learned not to be that way.[11]

Burdakin, too, was impatient, but his impatience was tempered and informed by his determination to follow the route he had always taken—to do the very best he could at whatever task he was given. It proved a most useful route, rewarded, as it was, by advancement to operating responsibilities at Buffalo, Baltimore, Pittsburgh, and Philadelphia.

All of this admittedly put stress on the Burdakin family (three moves in eleven months, as an example), but moving personnel was a long-standing tradition at Pennsylvania and within the industry generally. "That was the process by which the PRR developed their executives, and it took its toll. You were expected to be as dedicated to the railroad as you were to your family. It was just part of the culture. And it took a wife that would understand this, too. That was her job, and there were times when it might not be what she would like, but that was your part of the family plan and she would take care of the other family members. And so it required pretty strong solid people, dedicated people, and that is what they were looking for."[12]

"My evaluation of this moving around may seem, and certainly by today's standards, seems excessive, it was done at the time saying they wanted you to see different parts of the railroad and different operations. Really, that wasn't the advantage of moving around.

Time spent at Philadelphia for PRR was less than rewarding. Pennsy's GG1s labor at Jersey Meadows, December 1966. (Chris Burger photograph.)

The advantage was that you were forced into a situation of meeting entirely new people, both above you and below you, and you had to motivate both those people: your superiors and subordinates. And the education in how to get those people to do what you wanted them to do, or prove that the program you wanted was a good one. Or, if your superior says no, you have to go back and say what did I do wrong? The same thing is true for people beneath you. If you had a track foreman or yardmaster and you wanted a certain job done and he didn't do it the way you wanted, what did you do wrong? Why weren't you able to communicate your goals to him and motivate him to do it? That's where the true advantage of changing jobs and getting in different environments and different solutions. The true education of all that moving around, in my opinion, is the motivating and understanding of the people both above you and below you. As a result of that everybody that you worked for contributed to that education. Some of them were very strong, not only technically as far as how to do the job, but also how to handle people."[13]

Even as John Burdakin moved up the career ladder at PRR, the company accelerated its downward spiral. The causes were many and included managerial ossification as typified by Park Roeper and not attuned to change; a huge intercity and commuter passenger operation that garnered increasing chunks of red ink; subsidized modal competition such as the interstate highway system that particularly benefited the trucking industry, which ran off with a lot

John Burdakin moved from place to place across Pennsylvania's broad landscape. Heavy traffic at Horseshoe Curve always seemed awe-inspiring. August 1967. (Chris Burger photograph.)

of highly rated business; expansive urban terminal expenses; outdated and counterproductive labor agreements; and strangling government regulation at both state and federal levels. PRR's management in the late 1960s turned to the industry's favored elixir for relief: merger. Thus on February 1, 1968 was born Penn Central, a combination of Pennsylvania and archrival New York Central (into it was forced New York, New Haven & Hartford). Bankruptcy followed on June 21, 1970.

Penn Central's failure was easily predicted. Again the reasons were many but certainly included the clash of two very different corporate cultures—red (Pennsylvania) and green (New York Central). Even several months into the merger entire regions of the new company retained practices of earlier ownership. In any event, Burdakin moved about—to Pittsburgh and then to Cleveland as vice president and general manager and on to Detroit in the same capacity. At that level he was in a position to observe and evaluate those at the top—Stuart T. Saunders (PRR) and Alfred E. Perlman (NYC). Of the two, Burdakin had more contact with Perlman, whose responsibility included operations. Although Perlman is often cited with admiration, Burdakin had a mixed appraisal. He was "a great one to get out on the railroad," Burdakin said with respect, but he "was not as flexible as he should have been. He was stubborn, egotistical, and he often did not relate to the individual. He did look out for young bucks, get them to a certain point, and then threw them to the wolves." Perlman at one point argued that Penn Central and the industry at large needed no sales department if only the carriers delivered cars on time and to proper destinations. Burdakin's view was that it was more complicated than that. His assessment of Perlman might be written off as simply reflecting his strong feelings for PRR, which were palpable, though he had high praise for Robert G.

(Mike) Flannery who like Perlman came from NYC. Of the wreck of Penn Central, Burdakin would say: "It would make you vomit."[14]

To say that life at Penn Central was trying would be an acute understatement. Penn Central—PC—was derisively referred to as "Panic NYC." The ridiculous "green team" versus "red team" contest seemed endless at all levels, top to bottom. Nevertheless, Burdakin made impressive inroads with often deeply cynical contract people from both PRR and NYC backgrounds who tended to see him as "a good

This startling view at Cleveland from May 1965 suggests that PRR might indeed be the "standard railroad of the world" and "built for the ages." It was not so. (Chris Burger photograph.)

"When you switch out carelessness, you switch in safety" was a slogan winner at Penn Central. A proud Burdakin, second left, hands a $50 savings bond to the winner.

human being, a person to be trusted." Burdakin, whose identity with "red" Pennsylvania was well broadcast, nevertheless worked hard to build relationships with former NYC officers to overcome "grumble soup" and "bad blood" that so poisoned the waters. An example came when Burdakin's office car was parked in New York City at Grand Central Terminal. He asked Larry Baggerly, a former NYC officer, onto his car. It was a very simple act, but an act most uncommon in those wretched days at Penn Central—a member of one team actually conversing in a civil way with a member of the other team. Burdakin and Baggerly would see their paths cross again in the future. Baggerly recalled with a chuckle, "Burdakin treated NYC persons halfway decently. . . . he was a real gentleman."[15]

By now John Burdakin had been a railroad manager for more than two decades, and his philosophy and practice were well formed. He had a steely eye for operating efficiencies, a great devotion to "good track," and a clear view of "how to run the railroad." As to personnel and how he evaluated subordinates, he appeared stern with a right way/wrong way, black/white, book of rules mentality, but in fact, he was much more pragmatic. He was more willing in assessment to consider the impacts of events and circumstances on an individual and his family, as well as the ultimate needs of them and the company. Though he likely never said so, his internal compass firmly declared: "Rules cannot substitute for judgment."[16]

John Howard Burdakin was ready for the next opportunity or challenge.

Burdakin, center, had the opportunity to observe and evaluate Stuart T. Saunders, left, and Alfred E. Perlman, right, during his time at ill-fated Penn Central.

Chapter 4

Out of Canada

ONE OF THE MANY ISSUES THAT JOHN BURDAKIN CONFRONTED DURING HIS DETROIT time with Penn Central centered on the Detroit Terminal Railroad, jointly owned by Penn Central (née New York Central) and Grand Trunk Western (GTW). A Canadian, W. Douglas Piggott, represented GTW at the time, and the two men wrestled through several matters regarding Detroit Terminal. In the process, Piggott came to respect Burdakin, who must have confessed along the way that it was not enjoyable "working for a bankrupt carrier . . . worrying a lot about someone looking over your shoulder and asking what you were doing." Moreover, Burdakin and family—now fully developed with three boys (John, David, and Dan)—yearned for stability after seemingly moving from pillar to post and changing schools almost endlessly. Piggott, as it turned out, was close to retirement and, thinking well of Burdakin, passed his name to Robert A. Bandeen, a rising star at Canadian National (CN)—GTW's owner—in Montreal. Timing, as always, proved critical, since Bandeen and others at CN were brooding about the financial drag that Grand Trunk was on parent Canadian National.[1]

Burdakin was invited for an interview with Bandeen, who sketched out his concern that GTW eliminate losses and wean itself away "from CN's bank account," that it generate its own cash, and that he wanted "each successive year to be better than the one preceding." Burdakin asked Bandeen if he wanted each year better simply by deferring maintenance. For Burdakin that was the crucial question. The answer was no. Bandeen offered Burdakin the position of vice president of operations at GTW. Burdakin accepted.[2]

Was this a career cul de sac or even a trap? Would GTW offer security? Could Bandeen's requirements be met? The jury was out—and it would stay out for some while.

Canadian National in this era was a government-owned colossus that operated everything from hotels and railroads to an airline and an express company in Canada as well as Grand Trunk Western, Central Vermont (CV), and Duluth, Winnipeg & Pacific (DW&P) in the United States. Not surprisingly, senior management at Canadian National focused on "home properties," which were, after all, the core operations and were, at the same time, more likely to be scrutinized by members of Canada's Parliament. Consequently, Grand Trunk Western and the other U.S. holdings were viewed as comparatively insignificant and received attention accordingly. Indeed, the thought persisted at GTW that CN sent it only transient managers who were either on their way up at the parent company or on their way to oblivion. There were clues that CN looked on U.S. holdings as poor relatives unworthy of adequate and proper parental attention. And when GTW turned in a net annual deficit—which usually was the case—CN simply shrugged and covered the shortage. Small wonder that all of this was reflected on Grand Trunk Western in a general lack of cohesion, stability, and direction; in the categoric lack of incentive; and in low morale among middle managers who saw no hope of promotion or reward for innovation. This, in turn, was reflected by the road's dreary income statement.[3]

Staggering and seemingly endless shortfalls finally shook Montreal out of its lethargy. During the summer of 1966, directors of GTW were told that "Canadian National has been giving serious thought to various approaches that have been made . . . about the possibility of divesting its ownership of the Grand Trunk Western." CN managers were further jolted out of complacency by vociferous complaints from powerful General Motors Corporation (GM), which correctly argued that GTW's service had reached intolerably low levels—especially at Pontiac, Michigan, site of important GM plants whose rail transportation was supplied solely by GTW. Substantial annual deficits and inadequate service levels were no longer tolerable. Sale of the road was, of course, a possible avenue of resolution, but negotiations suggested that prospective buyers would not pay adequately for CN to recapture capital invested in GTW or even to meet "opportunity value" of the property. Another alternative had to be found.[4]

Grand Trunk's rather sterile-looking-general office building at 131 West Lafayette in downtown Detroit seemed to ooze a "This is the way we always have done it" mentality. John Burdakin would challenge that tradition.

Canadian National managers were jolted by vigorous complaints from General Motors, which argued that Grand Trunk service levels had dropped to intolerable levels.

Expansive internal debate continued. The options were frightfully few and mostly unattractive. Eventually, however, senior managers agreed to a concept of autonomy, and Robert A. Bandeen became the point man in developing an acceptable plan. Bandeen relished the opportunity. Outside attorneys urged creation of a holding company "in order to diversify into other business activities without the necessity of seeking Interstate Commerce Commission [ICC] approval." Why diversity? Bandeen knew that question was sure to surface internally and might even become a political question in Canada. Bankers were brought in. Kuhn Loeb advisors explained that the "choice is very significantly influenced by provisions of the U.S. federal income tax laws which permit an enterprise with tax losses to acquire profitable concerns and in effect, to operate them on a tax-free basis [in this case] until railroad-generated tax losses cease to be available."

This approach, they added, had been embraced earlier by Penn Central, Chicago & North Western, and Missouri-Kansas-Texas. Turning again to potential tax advantages, the bankers pointed out that CN might usefully choose to include another of its U.S. holdings—the increasingly prosperous Duluth, Winnipeg & Pacific, for example—as part of the holding company package. This could occur without ICC approval and would make it possible to utilize GTW's accumulated losses to offset DW&P profits. Creating a holding company simply for the purpose of evasion or avoidance of taxes could not be done, of course; CN's ultimate goal had to be creation of an affiliated group that eventually would generate a profit.[5]

To that end, Grand Trunk Industries was incorporated under Delaware law on September 22, 1970. Bandeen then suggested that "the name Grand Trunk Corporation [GTC] would be more appropriate and cause fewer problems in Washington and Ottawa." The change was made effective November 20. Meanwhile plans went forward under Bandeen's leadership to flesh out the holding company. Bandeen urged that Grand Trunk Corporation issue shares to acquire Grand Trunk Western and Duluth, Winnipeg & Pacific as well as Central Vermont. Beyond that Bandeen counseled creation under the holding company's banner of Grand Trunk Leasing Company "to take over equipment currently owned by CN and leased to GTW" and Grand Trunk Real Estate Company "to take over the non-rail assets of the rail subsidiaries." Bandeen was emphatic that the new holding company and "its various subsidiary companies will be separated from direct CN management" and that "American executives take over [management of] the various subsidiary corporations" and eventually the holding company itself.[6]

Events moved toward full fruition. Norman J. McMillan resigned as president of Grand Trunk Western in June 1971 and was succeeded by Bandeen (who continued as vice president of CN's important Great Lakes Region, to which GTW was physically connected). The entire package was completed on July 31 when GTW, DW&P, and CV passed to ownership of Grand Trunk Corporation—a wholly owned subsidiary of Canadian National.[7]

In a very real way Grand Trunk Corporation was the offspring of Robert A. Bandeen. His success or failure in bringing this child to maturity would be scrutinized carefully not only within the confines of CN's Montreal headquarters but from far afield as well. Among immediate problems and opportunities was the necessity of forging a senior management team that would be made up, Bandeen reminded Montreal, of railroaders from the United States. The immediate focus would be on Grand Trunk Western; Central Vermont and Duluth, Winnipeg & Pacific would continue temporarily under the management aegis of Canadian National. Bandeen considered three areas to be of crucial importance: operating, marketing, and finance. He chose for these John H. Burdakin, Walter H. Cramer, and Donald G. Wooden, respectively.

All three men, in one fashion or another, labored to create a new image—and self-image—of Grand Trunk Western. For example, GTW officers began to participate in the affairs of the Association of American Railroads, and Bandeen would sit on its board of directors. In addition, part of Cramer's marketing task was to advertise GTW as part of the much larger Canadian National and at the same time as a freestanding entity in the United States. Burdakin had the opportunity to physically change GTW's image. CN a decade earlier had abandoned its delightful and famous maple leaf logo in favor of an "elision of the letters CN into an attractive monogram that swam endlessly forward." GTW had reflected this change with its own GT logo, which Burdakin understood was not negotiable. But by employing approved CN colors in a new admixture, Burdakin reasoned that motive power and rolling stock could be adorned in a way to imply independence. Bandeen agreed. Locomotives quickly appeared in striking combination of blue, white, red/orange, and black; rolling stock showed up in blue. Wooden took up the essential task of creating new departments—accounting, finance, budgets and analysis, real estate, and tax—as well as fashioning appropriate procedures for each. He also set up a computer system adequate to the needs of GTW independent of CN.[8]

Robert A. Bandeen, left, was the architect of the Grand Trunk Corporation experiment. CN's Norman J. McMillan, right.

Burdakin, Cramer, and Wooden also turned to the business of establishing new practices and traditions. This would prove difficult. Burdakin, for instance, was astonished and dismayed to find steam locomotive parts stocked at the Battle Creek shops—a decade after the demise of steam. It reflected a deeper problem. Absentee or remote management had resulted in the absence of incentive across GTW. Montreal had not encouraged or rewarded innovation and creativity. As Don Wooden candidly observed: "Absentee management was no management." The new team constantly confronted profound cases of lethargy and suspicion. Its task was nothing less than transforming corporate culture.[9]

Burdakin's first chore was to get out on the property, to become familiar with it and its employees—to shake hands, to ask, "'What are you doing?,' to ask, 'How is it going?,' to be human." He found many officers and contract workers who were perfectly capable of doing their jobs, but a few personnel changes were essential. In all of this he would employ a firm but cautious approach. He would need to persuade and inspire goodwill at the same time, to present himself as a man of tenacity as well as fairness, to communicate energy and authority, to be candid and truthful so as to engender candor and truthfulness from subordinates. He had to be an agent of change, absolutely essential change, but it could not come as a rush else risk a counterproductive backlash. He would labor to create an atmosphere of encouragement, innovation, and ingenuity that over time would motivate subordinates to become problem solvers willing to attack large, apparently intractable problems. None of the serious issues

In addition to John Burdakin, Robert A. Bandeen chose Donald G. Wooden and Walter H. Cramer to complete senior management at Detroit.

confronting Grand Trunk Western could be solved totally at the top of management pyramid; Burdakin understood the need for teamwork and a capacity to learn from the past, to learn from mistakes, and to move forward with insight and fortitude. Overly forceful bosses, he had learned, ran the risk of turning subordinates into patsies or sycophants; consensus-obsessed bosses could institutionalize dithering; micromanagers tended to neglect the big picture. The right and proper ingredients were good character, common sense, and especially judgment— judgment to know when to modulate and when to pull out all stops.

Upon arriving at GTW, Burdakin declared that he had confidence in all hands and that he needed all hands for the tasks ahead. Such evenhanded, across-the-board determination not to assign blame for GTW's past performance but to treat everyone the same going forward proved a much-needed tonic. Burdakin conveyed his expectations clearly and firmly from top to bottom, and Burdakin himself set the example of hard work, competence, and pride in oneself that he expected others to follow. Leadership, he understood, was a matter of picking good people and helping them do their best. Attributes of loyalty, discipline, and devotion to duty on the part of subordinates had to be matched by patience, tolerance, and understanding on the part of leaders. The GTW family quickly deduced that there was not a phony bone in Burdakin's body. His approach was completely transparent, firm, frank, and fair. "Don't step on toes any more than you want your own toes stepped on" seemed John Burdakin's equivalent of the Golden Rule.[10]

In a few instances Burdakin found need to seriously get the attention of subordinates and even change personnel. The trainmaster at Flint contended that he could "make do" with a broken stepladder, but Burdakin saw it as a reflection of a poor attitude toward safe practice. "I had to raise my voice with him," Burdakin recalled. When the superintendent at Battle Creek was enjoying a Saturday evening square dance instead of attending to a main-line derailment, Burdakin determined that he needed a new superintendent at Battle Creek. And when the chief engineer did not comply with Burdakin's command to use tie plates when replacing ties, Burdakin replaced him.[11]

John Burdakin recalled that Bandeen was willing to wait as long as the current year was better than the last. As it developed, 1973 was vastly better than 1972. Indeed, GTC posted a net income of $3.9 million. Unfortunately, the future looked much less promising, and in fact, the United States slid into a severe recession with curtailed demand for automobiles, durable goods, and housing materials. The recession was exacerbated by an energy crisis—the oil shock—and severe inflation.[12]

All of these circumstances put great pressure on Grand Trunk Western and on John Burdakin, who by then was the company's executive vice president. The new team had succeeded in driving down GTW's operating ratio (ratio of operating expenses to operating revenues) from 90.3 in 1971 to 82.2 in 1973. This had been accomplished in part by cutting jobs, which, predictably, had gone down badly with labor leaders. To be sure, Burdakin had crossed swords with labor shortly after he arrived in 1971 when he abolished yard assignments at Christmastime. That had resulted in pickets at the general office building in downtown Detroit, and headlines in one newspaper that read "Burdakin Kills Santa Claus." In fact, the automobile industry routinely shut down from Christmas Eve until the day after New Year's, leaving several GTW yard crews without meaningful work. The tradition under Canadian managers had been to call these crews anyway, but Burdakin saw it only as a waste and unnecessary expense—intolerable given the company's awful financial performance. The Christmas incident simply reflected a deeper problem. Labor leaders had long since learned that GTW, managed at a distance and dependent as it had become on the automobile industry, would cave in if workers slowed service to and from General Motors plants. The tradition was firm: upon interruption of service or even a slowdown, GM officials contacted Montreal and GTW managers were told to yield. By 1971, however, competitive pressures were so intense and GTW's financial position so precarious that Burdakin—with Bandeen's clear support—determined that this tradition had to go. The problem, in many ways, was one of communication. "We might argue how to carve up the pie," Burdakin said of contract forces at GTW, "but we had to find agreement on how to make a good pie." Burdakin sent a strong message that he intended to be firm, but he also promised to be candid and fair. He joined with Bandeen, Cramer, and Wooden in touring the property and in meeting with the various crafts. He also authorized expenditures for corporate communications as well as an annual "Santa Train," designed to open up avenues of communication "and to tell employees that their job efforts are appreciated." Still and all, Burdakin insisted that "business as usual" was not good enough. To cling to old ways, if those old ways were unproductive, was to invite extinction. Change was painful, but change was essential. It came, if grudgingly, and over time was typified by closer relations with employees and their unions.[13]

One major drain on GTW had passed. The "passenger problem" ended with the establishment of the National Railway Passenger Corporation (Amtrak) on May 1, 1971. Amtrak determined to omit GTW routes (Port Huron–Chicago, Detroit-Chicago) from its national

General Motors routinely shut down from Christmas Eve until the day after New Year's. Should GTW do the same?

network. Final runs were made on April 30, 1971. GTW was obliged to purchase $2.1 million of Amtrak stock, and $2.5 million in expenses were charged against 1971 income as extraordinary items. Passenger equipment leased from CN was returned and, significantly, twenty locomotives were converted to freight service—negating for the time being the need to order new freight power. If the intercity passenger service ended, the commuter problem—three daily trains, except Saturday and Sunday, in each direction between Detroit and Pontiac—persisted.[14]

A corollary issue was the matter of properties held by Chicago & Western Indiana Railroad (C&WI) of which GTW was part owner. C&WI dated from June 2, 1879. It had been purchased shortly thereafter by a consortium of roads that had equal rights to common property in and about Chicago. Included was Dearborn Station, made redundant by Amtrak's decision to centralize its Chicago operations at Union Station. Dearborn and other nearby C&WI properties had great real estate potential encumbered by collective ownership that was not overcome until 1975. The remaining C&WI operations were conducted on a user-shared-cost basis.[15]

Grand Trunk Corporation came through the 1973–1974 recession surprisingly well. Carloadings were down, but revenues turned upward because of the Interstate Commerce Commission approved rate increases. At GTW, John Burdakin diligently labored to control costs by way of extended shop closings, force reductions, and operating efficiencies. Deficits were reduced annually from 1971 through 1975; in the latter year the shortfall was $7.2 million, the lowest in nineteen years. GTC showed net profits of $6.65 million in 1974 and $4.251 million in 1975.[16]

The *Santa Train* was designed to "tell employees that their job efforts are appreciated."

Meanwhile, Canadian National's Norman J. MacMillan faced retirement. Among those rumored to be in the running as MacMillan's replacement was Robert A. Bandeen, who, on May 1, 1972, had moved back to Montreal as executive vice president—remaining as president of Grand Trunk Corporation and firmly in control of that experiment. The early positive results from GTC likely prompted Canadian prime minister Pierre Trudeau to appoint the forty-three-year-old Bandeen as president and chief executive officer of CN effective May 1, 1974.[17]

What ramifications, if any, did this development have for GTC and its constituent properties? Most of all, it implied continuing and even greater support for the holding company. It also implied managerial alterations. In 1971, Bandeen had pledged that an American would head GTC once it was on its feet. During the months and years following he had watched the "little group" of senior managers in Detroit with a keen eye. Which one of them would be the best choice to advance up the ladder? Bandeen bet on John Burdakin, who was named to head Grand Trunk Western effective October 1, 1974.[18]

Matters shifted by degree. Separately organized companies—GTW, DW&P, and CV along with their subsidiaries—were included under the GTC canopy, although the early focus was on GTW. Operating and capital budgets of all were included in GTC reports. In that sense, GTC was, as Bandeen said, "a shell operation, without much substance," except that as a holding company it could file a consolidated tax return sheltering income from profitable properties with losses from Grand Trunk Western.[19]

The *Santa Train* at South Bend, Indiana, December 14, 1975. (David Korkhouse photograph.)

The most profitable property was Duluth, Winnipeg & Pacific, no longer a logging road or a sleepy branch but now a funnel for increasingly heavy traffic moving from central and western Canada into the United States. CN managers designed a calculated campaign to improve DW&P's track structure, but not in a way that would deny profit so necessary to Bandeen's holding company strategy. Net income for the period 1971–1975, inclusive, averaged $3.146 million annually. Principal commodities handled included lumber, potash, and paper and wood pulp.[20]

Central Vermont, by comparison, was a sometimes performer. It had turned in net losses from 1968 through 1970, but from 1971 to 1974, inclusive, boasted average annual net income of $699,250. Red ink returned in 1975, however. CV found itself serving a region that was overbuilt with rail lines given modal competition, that was losing its industrial base, and that increasingly embraced an antibusiness climate. Gross ton-miles reflected this—dropping from over one billion in 1968 to 642 million in 1975. Average tons per train remained constant; no efficiencies were produced in that important category. The number of employees fell from 680 in 1968 to 439 in 1975, a number easily adequate to handle business, but the rapid decline caused consternation among employees, who recalled a more robust era not so long ago. Amtrak reinstituted passenger service in 1972 above White River Junction as part of a New York City–Montreal route, but now more freight moved inbound from Canada than outbound. The future of Central Vermont looked distressingly problematic, but Bandeen wondered if a shake-up similar to that under way at GTW would produce similar results for CV. With that in mind, and to reestablish executive authority in St. Albans, Bandeen dispatched Donald Wooden as executive vice president in March 1974.[21]

GTW owned impressive properties in Detroit that were coveted by others. A mutually advantageous deal was struck in 1973–75 in which the railroad vacated much of its waterfront yard.

Another, if quite unheralded, subsidiary of Grand Trunk Corporation was Grand Trunk Leasing (GTL), to which rolling stock leased by GTW was transferred on January 1, 1972. Thereafter all interest, principal, and rental payments were rendered to the subsidiary. DW&P and CV later became parties, and GTL also expanded into leases of motive power. The arrangement was profitable from the start. They offered additional advantages, such as the ability to raise capital from financing its lien-free rolling stock. Additionally, GTL provided a means of separating rolling stock from the constituent railroads if any or all were disposed of.[22]

In announcing Robert A. Bandeen's appointment as president of Canadian National, the *GT Reporter* asserted that "the separately incorporated Canadian National properties in the United States" had been revitalized. That overstated reality. But Bandeen's concept of a holding company had been validated, and a strong management team had been established for Grand Trunk Western. Bandeen clearly had constructed a firm foundation, and a crucial lesson had been learned: change was necessary to survive in a changed and changing world. If Grand Trunk Corporation was to survive—let alone prosper—its managers would have to be nimble. And Montreal must allow them to be nimble—nay, Montreal must demand it.[23]

Chapter 5

A Patient Approach

Robert A. Bandeen made bold plans for Canadian National, which enunciated with equal vigor and directness. A new management organization went into effect on January 1, 1976. "Underlying current corporate planning," said Bandeen, "is the conviction that the best interests of Canada are served when the company is able to conduct its operations on a commercial basis." Bandeen recognized that CN was altogether too conservative and traditional in its business posture and modus operandi, and that its organizational structure and traditional operation resembled a stodgy government bureaucracy. His alterations were designed to give the company "the flexibility to adapt to changing market demands and financial conditions." The new plan was based on the profit center concept and included five operating divisions to manage major revenue-producing activities. The object, said Bandeen, was to "simplify the administration of CN and improve the efficiency and profitability of its various divisions."[1]

Bandeen warmed to his subject. "In the economic and political climate of today, the role of CN as a profit-seeking business corporation is by no means incompatible with acknowledged public service obligations of the company. Indeed, business efficiency enhances CN's ability to supply any public service required of it fully and well and as economically as possible." That meant, Bandeen said bluntly, that the company would have to reduce costs, increase productivity, and generate more revenues. The entire package mirrored Bandeen's philosophy and his experience with Grand Trunk Corporation.[2]

Bandeen was the right man for CN at the right time. Canada was increasingly willing to acknowledge that the transportation climate had changed and with it CN's role. Bandeen liked to find solutions to problems; he was imaginative, aggressive, and ambitious; and he had fixed ideas about what he wanted to do and how to do it—fast. Within the headquarters building and abroad, Bandeen set a dynamic tone. While he understood the company's roots and would be informed by the company's history, he would not be controlled by it. For example, CN was dominated by its operating department, hardly unusual in the North American rail industry at the time, but pronounced at CN. Bandeen recognized this domination, saw its shortcomings, and challenged the tradition. He was similarly put off by arrogance in the traffic department, the mentality of which he sarcastically summarized: "If it doesn't go in a boxcar, carry it yourself." Those who craved constancy were uncomfortable with Bandeen, for change would typify his watch.[3]

Bandeen would have his hands full. In the 1960s CN had produced more than $413 million in deficits and had earned surplus before interest charges only in 1960 and 1961.

Robert A. Bandeen made bold plans for Canadian National just as he had for CN's properties in the United States.

Employment had been pared from 104,155 in 1960 to 84,388 in 1969, but the company's operating ratio averaged a dismal 99.43 for the decade. CN's performance during the early part of the 1970s was little better. Deficits for the years 1970–1975 were more than $47 million, and the operating ratio averaged 99.62.[4]

John Burdakin developed an intense admiration for Bandeen and learned much from him—especially in the areas of strategic planning, finance, political intercourse, and framing and understanding "the big picture." "He was the finest executive I ever had the pleasure of working for—in fact he was the finest executive I ever met." Small wonder. Formed by his southern Ontario farm background and his Presbyterian upbringing, the railroad and later insurance industries offered him success in business, and the arts fed his soul; he was a season ticket holder for the opera and for the theater, and he was a regular attendee at symphonies. His well-roundedness helped shape him as a businessman who chose analysis over antagonism. He asked employees to explain succinctly what they needed to get the job done. When they presented him with a proposal, he would ask a few questions and deliver a quick yes or no, or ask for a rewrite. Colleagues and subordinates in the main expressed gratitude for a boss who offered a steady hand and an open mind.[5]

As Robert Bandeen labored to redefine the way Canadian National addressed its business, he increasingly trusted John H. Burdakin to do the same at Grand Trunk Western. Bandeen reminded Burdakin that the circumstances at GTW were very much like those of its parent; like CN, it had to reduce costs, increase productivity, and generate more revenue. Yet there were differences. CN had much longer average hauls and relatively less competition. For GTW there remained the uncompromising demand to maintain high-speed, high-capacity plant in the short Chicago–Port Huron / Chicago-Detroit corridors while supplying very demanding on-line customers with saturated gathering and distribution services—all of it in a fiercely competitive environment featuring multiple modes, especially in Michigan, a state that never saw a roadway or a multiple-axle truck it did not admire.

Burdakin's charge from Bandeen was to effect change at GTW. Change, however, meant alteration of the status quo—disruptive, painful, and emotional. Such, for example, was the case with line abandonments. A CN team in 1969 had urged scrutiny of a full 240 miles of

GTW had very demanding online customers with saturated gathering and distribution requirements.

line, branches, or segments of branches, all in Michigan. Internal studies were initiated before Burdakin arrived, and abandonments were prosecuted by him as data showed clear deficits from operations and as the political climate allowed. First to go was a portion of GTW's Jackson line, thirty-five miles. More wrenching was a decision in 1974 to seek termination of the westernmost section of the Grand Haven line; final runs came on July 20, 1977, between Coopersville and Grand Haven, fifteen miles. Burdakin took no pleasure in abandonments, but neither did he apologize: "We have an obligation to the people of Michigan and our customers not to waste our resources on continued maintenance and operation of lines which, despite our best efforts, produce net deficits."[6]

Line abandonment was an issue that always charged emotions and carried political risk. GTW's deficit-ridden car ferry operation on Lake Michigan was even more difficult. Ferrying cars had the very real advantage of avoiding the always congested Chicago gateway, of saving ton-miles, and of expediting time-sensitive shipments. Unfortunately, ferrying operations also were extremely labor intensive—a vexing problem exacerbated by escalating wage scales and expanded modal competition.[7]

By the late 1960s, CN analysts predicted a savings of at least $1 million annually if GTW dropped service. These same analysts recognized, however, that the issue was complex. Cross-lake tonnage for GTW aggregated 833,000 in 1967 and 800,000 in 1968 and included significant blocks of auto frames and beer moving eastbound, Canadian newsprint moving westbound,

GTW's Lake Michigan car ferry operation was a distinct financial drag.

and local movements of industrial sand and coke between Milwaukee and Muskegon. Any cost-benefit analysis was obligated to consider water operations plus terminal costs in Milwaukee as well as the lengthy branch to Muskegon against system benefits to GTW and CN.[8]

GTW managers looked for options. The company's three vessels—*Grand Rapids* (1926), *Madison* (1927), and *City of Milwaukee* (1931)—could be modernized to make them less labor-intensive, or new vessels could be acquired. Neither alternative could be justified, however, on a capital-reward basis. Burdakin ordered further study, pointing out the need to protect, as much as possible, important traffic emanating from Milwaukee or passing overhead.[9]

James L. Elliott, general manager of the car ferry company, prepared an impressive proposal for survival in 1972. Elliott's proposal might have been implemented had GTW been flush; it was not flush. Loaded cars handled by ferry in 1971 dropped to 10,900, requiring only one round trip daily. The sharp recession and fuel crisis of 1973 and 1974 hastened a decision. On May 21, 1974, GTW's board authorized "whatever action . . . deemed necessary and prudent to relieve the company of the economic burden of continuing operation of the Grand Trunk–Milwaukee Car Ferry Company." Papers were filed with the ICC on February 14, 1975. Said the plainspoken Burdakin: "The use of a 242-ton ferry manned by a 34-man crew to move 22 rail cars across Lake Michigan is now too costly to meet the competition." While the ICC dallied, losses increased: $1.1 million in 1974, $1.3 million in 1975, $1.6 million in 1976. Authorization for termination of service finally arrived, and when the

Discontinuance of the car ferry would be a long, tedious, but essential task.

City of Milwaukee tied up at Muskegon at 1:08 A.M. on October 31, 1978, GTW wrote finis to an important chapter of its history.[10]

Burdakin understood that it was not enough simply to trim; prosperity for Grand Trunk Western could not be achieved merely by reducing operations. It was, as always, necessary to spend money to make money. Conservative by nature, Burdakin weighed his monetary resources, husbanded them, and spent only when and where he was convinced there was promise of return. Track structure, he firmly believed, required constant attention and upgrading to provide the thoroughfare adequate to high-speed needs of GTW customers. The road had less than 75 miles of continuous-welded rail when he arrived in 1971, but over the next nine years GTW installed 161 miles of it, averaging 17.9 miles in good years and bad. Additional impressive expenditures went for mechanized track machines, steel bridges, extended passing tracks, lengthened yard tracks, power switches and heaters, ties and anchors, hot box detectors, and centralized traffic control. Burdakin was properly pleased by the campaign. In 1975, GTW—with Burdakin's enthusiastic blessing—began to advertise itself as the "Good Track Road." The motto was hardly whimsical. "It is a challenge to everyone on the railroad," said Burdakin, "because any shortcomings in track maintenance, or employee performance, or customer service can mar the reputation gained." The "Good Track" concept derived in part from Burdakin's engineering background and his experience at Penn Central, where property conditions had rapidly deteriorated, and in part from his knowledge that nervous customers were moving

GTW finally wrote finis to the car ferry chapter of its history on October 31, 1978.

away from rail transport because of poor track conditions and correspondingly poor service on many eastern and Midwestern carriers. Shippers and other railroads quickly took note of GTW's "Good Track" pledge and applauded. "[GTW] is a hell of a good railroad; they have a good piece of track and they work at it," said Denver & Rio Grande Western's G. B. Aydelott.[11]

An adequate and well-maintained stable of motive power was similarly required to move freight on demanding schedules. The motive power fleet when Burdakin arrived was made up mostly of models from General Motor's Electro-Motive Division (EMD). When second-generation units arrived, they came from EMD in high-horsepower models and later in the form of utilitarian 2,000-horsepower GP-38s.[12]

Rolling stock needs were constant and varied to reflect the demands of GTW's largest customers. New boxcars, flats, trilevel auto racks, airslide covered hoppers, and cabooses were procured by lease, leveraged lease, and conditional sales agreement. Shop forces at Port Huron repeatedly proved their mettle by "stretching" boxcars, by converting auto racks into trailer-on-flat-car flats, by making ballast cars out of covered hoppers, and by maintaining the entire ten-thousand-car fleet. Ownership of equipment held by Grand Trunk Leasing passed to GTW on January 1, 1976, and GTW then entered into informal lease arrangements with Central Vermont and Duluth, Winnipeg & Pacific for the same stock. This resulted in increased depreciation and interest expense but was offset by reduced rental costs. Grand Trunk Leasing was then dissolved by merging it into Grand Trunk Corporation.[13]

Grand Trunk
the Good Track road

John Burdakin would make good on his "Good Track" pledge.

Robert A. Bandeen, on the ground, John Burdakin, top running board, and others took pleasure in welcoming new motive power at GTW.

Shop forces at Port Huron repeatedly proved their mettle by "stretching" boxcars, converting auto racks into TOFC flats, and maintaining the entire fleet of rolling stock.

Events surrounding the Pontiac-Detroit commuter operation took a curious path. The three trains in each direction daily except Sunday were a constant financial drain. Any attempt to discontinue them was bound to arouse public hostility, but Burdakin stated emphatically that "the deficit operation must be eliminated." Fortunately, GTW avoided a public relations disaster when a bargain was struck with the Southeastern Michigan Transportation Authority to assume responsibility for the service effective December 19, 1973.[14]

Other matters in the Detroit area also came under close scrutiny. The Detroit Terminal Railroad Company, a switching operation and owned in equal shares by GTW and Penn Central, suffered progressive losses—$118,000 in 1971 and $102,000 in 1972. These were only the most recent in an unbroken string from 1956. Bandeen sought to sell GTW's interest to Penn Central, and negotiations to that end ebbed and flowed until Penn Central disappeared. Consolidated Rail Corporation (Conrail), successor to many Penn Central properties, including one-half interest in Detroit Terminal, renewed negotiations. For GTW, Detroit Terminal's primary value derived from a connection it provided with Detroit, Toledo & Ironton (DT&I), but GTW—under provisions of the final system plan defining Conrail—gained a new and more direct connection with DT&I through Conrail itself. Consequently, Detroit Terminal was a cash drain and became operationally redundant. GTW finally dumped its interest in 1981.[15]

John Burdakin, right, was delighted to shed responsibility for Detroit–Pontiac commuter operations.

Robert Bandeen, who had "wanted to take a whole new look at things" when he was appointed president of Grand Trunk Corporation, took the same approach at Canadian National. His profit center concept, introduced at GTC, was fully implemented at CN. And in a bold attempt to generate adequate data for interpretation and to develop an efficient car-handling policy, Bandeen authorized huge expenditures for a new, online computer system styled after Southern Pacific's famous TOPS. Important indices reflected improvement. Freight car productivity increased one-quarter from 1974 to 1978; gross tons per employee rose by 3.9 percent per year in the same period; and the operating ratio approached 90.0 by the end of the decade.[16]

As Bandeen struggled with the Canadian National labyrinth, he increasingly gave authority to John Burdakin for matters related to Grand Trunk Corporation. Indeed, Burdakin became president of the holding company on January 1, 1976. At the same time, Bandeen and Burdakin agreed that it was time to integrate Central Vermont and Duluth, Winnipeg & Pacific more fully into GTC's orbit. Consequently, management agreements with CN were dropped, and Burdakin appointed Gerald L. Maas as general manager of CV and Phillip C. Larson as general manager for DW&P.[17]

Integrating CV and DW&P more fully into GTC, Bandeen and Burdakin agreed, meant that the two roads—like GTW—needed to develop independent personalities. Neither man viewed integration as contradictory. Rather, both agreed that management decisions should be made locally—at St. Albans and Duluth, not at Detroit or Montreal. There would be oversight, to be sure, but they predicted that initiative and independence would result in greater productivity.

Donald Wooden had already done much to put a stamp of independence on CV. Maas, who followed Wooden, continued and expanded the process. Train dispatching, for example, returned to St. Albans from Montreal. This was more than symbolic. It reflected Maas's determination to make the company "a stand-alone railroad." Run-through train operations were perfected between Montreal and Washington in cooperation with CN, Boston & Maine, and Conrail; CV's marketing arm was reorganized to aggressively seek new business; and the property was spruced up. The campaign was striking in its completeness and in its effectiveness. Burdakin's pleasure was reflected when he promoted Maas to general manager of GTW. Larson moved from DW&P to CV as successor to Maas, and Jerome F. Corcoran—formerly director of budgets and cost analysis at GTW—moved to DW&P.[18]

Wooden, Maas, and then Larson pumped vitality into Central Vermont. New sales offices were established in Toronto and New London; CV eagerly solicited newsprint to Florida destinations and established impressive online distribution centers; trackmen installed the first welded rail (and the first in the state of Vermont); and a new intermodal train entered service. Employment in 1976 was only 60 percent of 1968, but morale was strong; CV won the E. H. Harriman Bronze Medal for its safety record in 1976. And the road repainted one of its diesel units in a bold patriotic style to commemorate the nation's bicentennial.[19]

Central Vermont developed its own character. Its historic and comely general office building at St. Albans overlooked the passage of trains.

The record of Duluth, Winnipeg & Pacific was less complex and more profitable. As with CV, it gained more autonomy in 1976, with accountability resting with managers appointed by GTC. Unlike CV, however, marketing and sales responsibilities remained with Canadian National; GTW would provide other "services, counsel, advice, and expertise" under management contract. DW&P's compact operation simply did not require "hiring and maintaining a large staff of its own for such purposes." With low overhead costs and with a narrow but lucrative traffic base, it earned impressive profits during the last half of the 1970s—$3.67 million was the low for the period, in 1975, and $8 million was the high, in 1978.[20]

DW&P's performance was impressive by most standards. Gross ton-miles escalated, as did average tons per train; at the same time, the operating ratio steadied at a most agreeable 65.9 average for the last half of the decade. Productivity improved perceptibly in 1976 when agreement with labor organizations allowed the company to eliminate Virginia, Minnesota, as a crew change point. Subsequently crews ran through from Duluth to Ranier, across from Fort Frances, Ontario. Running through was made possible by agreements with the unions and significant expenditures to upgrade track structure with heavy welded rail, deep ballast, and thousands of ties. By the end of 1976, a 45-mile-per-hour track speed was afforded over most of the line. Employee numbers sagged, but morale remained high; DW&P ranked high in safety among railroads of its size. The road's new motto, "DW&P—Delivered With Pride," was as much fact as long term aspiration."[21]

Of the Grand Trunk Corporation's railroad properties, DW&P might be the least remarked, but it assuredly became the financial star; CV and GTW were the problematic financial performers. Yet because of its size and scope of operation, GTW always demanded greatest attention. Burdakin's formula for the company was characteristically direct: advanced marketing and energetic sales coupled with aggressive cost control. Easily enough said. As always, however, GTW was pressured by powerful shippers that demanded a fleet of often expensive and specialized equipment with dependable high-speed service in a corridor always characterized by profound competition. Of challenges there were plenty.

Walter Cramer, with John Burdakin's full backing, continued his campaign to seek, hold, and expand volume. His work gained respect for GTW across the industry. At Burlington Northern, Thomas J. Lamphier said: "He is one of the first real marketers in our business, and he understands all concepts." James R. Sullivan at Conrail noted that GTW was not a leader in rate-making because of its relatively small size, but he considered it "a responsible organization" and certainly "not a patsy." Generally speaking, said Sullivan, "I am quite favorably impressed with GTW." In 1974 it garnered the American Railway Development Association's outstanding marketing achievement designation by reclaiming shipments of iron and steel previously lost to truckers. Four years later GTW earned *Modern Railroads'* Silver Freight Car Award for its imaginative and aggressive "Tank Train" package to move residual oil on behalf of Michigan's Consumers Power Company.[22]

One area of important potential growth was intermodal—piggybacking trailers and containers on flat cars. As volume grew, thirty-five acres of land were acquired in Chicago to provide a modern facility at that critical juncture. The $2.5 million "GT Railport," opened in the fall of 1975, reflected expanded service to Detroit, Toronto, and Montreal, and to and from Halifax in conjunction with transatlantic steamship interests. The expenditure seemed justified given the 120 percent increase in intermodal business at Chicago in 1976 over 1975. Detroit's Ferndale Yard was also modified to handle expanded volumes. "MoTerm"—a thirteen-acre, $1.5 million facility—opened for business late in 1976 and was expanded in 1978. GTW

GTW was pressured by powerful shippers that demanded a fleet of often expensive and specialized equipment.

claimed to offer the lowest ramp-to-ramp rates, an unmatched availability of equipment, and the fastest and most reliable service in the Detroit-Chicago corridor. Indeed, intermodal volume between those points increased by 96 percent in 1978, and a year later the company operated two daily dedicated intermodal trains in each direction on that run. The financial reward from all of this was unclear, however.[23]

Early in 1975, John Burdakin enumerated GTW's objectives. The first goal, he said, was to "direct the activities of the company so as to achieve a long term profitable position reflecting adequate return on assets and to attain fiscal stability and independence in terms of cash for operating and capital expenditures." The statement was short and direct—characteristic of Burdakin. Yet GTW was a high-cost railroad with a limited revenue stream. Burdakin's aspiration would be difficult to achieve.[24]

The task of making Grand Trunk Western a more efficient property rested primarily with Burdakin and those who followed him in the operating department. The road was small enough "to get your arms around," but it was no "mom and pop operation." Its locomotive fleet during the 1970s averaged 191 units, its rolling stock for the same period averaged 10,278 cars, and the road produced prodigious ton-miles—nearly nine billion for 1978, as an example. Employment averaged 4,548 per year. The numbers were impressive. But so were the problems, especially GTW's vest pocket route structure, which did not provide long

GT Railport was unveiled with appropriate ceremony in the fall of 1975. Chicago mayor Richard J. Daley is shown here with an outsized key to symbolize the opening. Burdakin is on the left, and Bandeen is looking on at center.

hauls to offset staggering costs of gathering and distributing. The operating ratio averaged a disappointing 109 for the 1970s. Nevertheless, Burdakin's nostrums—weight reduction with complimentary bodybuilding exercises—were bearing fruit. GTW's losses in 1976 were $1.7 million, the lowest in twenty years. Moreover, GTW earned net profit of $18.6 million during the final three years of the decade.[25]

Such good news traveled rapidly, as might be expected. "It is not true that GTW is doomed to be a succession of mounting deficits, service deterioration and eventual bankruptcy," wrote Gus Welty in *Railway Age*. Indeed, "GTW has come a long way toward a U.S. orientation in the way it's managed, compared with the way it was run (more or less as a CN afterthought) for the first 40-plus years of its existence." Tom Shedd, at *Modern Railroads*, also took note of the "turnaround now under way at GTW" and concluded that "Canadian National made a wise decision in freeing its U.S. subsidiaries to do their own thing—and in bringing in American operating, financial and marketing officers to lead." Moreover, Shedd observed, "GTW has become a lively, competitive, full-fledged member of the U.S. railroad industry." Still another writer noted that "Burdakin has a management team that takes second place to nobody in its enthusiasm for the job at hand, with a work force that seems to take equal pride in what's happening." Burdakin properly shared such accolades. "My personal pride in the corporation comes from pride within the company. Our improved financial picture reflects the activities of those employees."[26]

Nobody was happier than Robert A. Bandeen and John Burdakin. Grand Trunk Corporation, they gleefully observed, produced net profit after the second year of existence and for the decade of the 1970s earned an admirable $53.8 million. In some years, all three railroads—GTW, CV, and DW&P—were profitable on a stand-alone basis. Furthermore, Bandeen reminded, since its inception in 1971, GTC had filed a consolidated federal income tax return with its subsidiaries, which took into account previous operating losses. As the corporation looked to the new decade, $16.4 million in investment tax credit carryovers, expiring in various amounts through 1986, were available to reduce taxes payable. Bandeen's vision—his experiment—had been vindicated. But there were new problems, strategic in some cases, and a new competitive environment to understand and to respond to. Managers would have to be nimble of mind and fleet of foot if GTC was to bear full flower in the 1980s.[27]

Chapter 6

Taking Stock

BY THE HOLIDAY SEASON OF 1976, JOHN BURDAKIN HAD BEEN AT GRAND TRUNK FOR a half-decade. It was time to take stock. Performance and station of necessity would be measured twofold: against the North American railroad industry at large and against Bandeen's broad calculation to Americanize Canadian National's holdings in the United States.

For most Americans in or near the railroad industry—investors, managers, contract employees, customers—the decade of the 1970s was a bad dream, a time willingly forgotten. Indeed, many observers, and perhaps most, thought the industry had seen its best years. Others of a darker mood were ready to toss railroads into the dustbin of history. The awful wreckage of Penn Central and then failure of several other northeastern carriers and growing malaise among railroads in the heartland coupled with the energy crisis of 1974 finally resulted in action at the federal level. Congress then brought forth various pieces of legislative relief. The creation of Conrail in 1976 reflected as much. Into Conrail were poured ashes of Penn Central and various flotsam and jetsam but blessed with rights and privileges as yet not fully understood. Burdakin was guarded in his assessment of Conrail and of its potential one way or another. He did warn CN's board of directors that Conrail represented "a large government supported carrier . . . a new formidable competition . . . that will have the ability to draw on huge amounts of government funds and emphasize services at any cost rather than being based upon economy of operation." And, of course, the American railroad industry remained shackled by the regulatory intransigence of the Interstate Commerce Commission, a poster child of government ineptitude. Despite all of this, John Burdakin remained bullish on the railroad industry and the Grand Trunk properties within it. Was he simply Pollyanna-ish? Absolutely not. "We are not looking to the past except as a foundation for building and an inspiration for the future," said the feisty Burdakin.[1]

Robert A. Bandeen remained, as he always would be, Burdakin's mentor—teaching, teaching, teaching, and Burdakin learning, learning, learning. In Bandeen Burdakin saw "an extremely talented individual with a great presence, tremendous presence, and a good solid intellect, not being one to fly into directions haphazardly or quickly. He knew where he wanted to go, knew how to get there and would be willing to, as long as you're making progress, watch that progress toward the goal he had set. He would be able to visualize the pluses and minuses and what was going on, very quickly asked pointed questions. He would say, yes, that's a direction we ought to go. If not, or no, we ought to go some other direction, or I don't think we ought to proceed, that decision would come in one telephone call. But no action was taken by Grand Trunk that did not have Bandeen's knowledge. We never surprised Bandeen. We did some things and we surprised a lot of staff up there with the things we did, but we did not surprise Bandeen."[2]

Bandeen approved of and supported Burdakin's implementation of the Americanization plan. Burdakin's impression on arriving had been that "GTW did not get proper attention out of Montreal . . . that Grand Trunk got to be very much the low end of the totem pole . . . that if the little people wanted to do something, it was extremely difficult to get approval from anybody above them . . . that the little wheel couldn't turn the big wheel . . . that it wasn't worthwhile to become innovative 'cause you couldn't get it done anyway because you couldn't get the boss to approve it." The result was stagnation—intolerable stagnation. "There had to be change."[3]

Change there was. By this time Burdakin had in place a management team that "took second place to nobody in its enthusiasm for the job at hand and a workforce that took pride in what was happening." To be sure, Burdakin emphasized human intangibles such as pride, initiative, ambition, and determination to inspire superior performance from Grand Trunk personnel. "I prefer working through people, developing their initiative, motivating them, expanding their horizons," he explained. "You have to be open and aboveboard with employees, give them encouragement and hope." With good people and with the right spirit, said Burdakin, "We cannot fail to achieve whatever goal we set." Moreover, "We can face the stern duties ahead because we have honorably met our past obligations." And to members of the Grand Trunk Corporation board and to senior members of the management team Burdakin's feelings of respect and appreciation were fully transparent. "I have no way of telling you how much I appreciate your interest, your dedication and your friendship. It has been a distinct honor and privilege to work for and serve as president of Grand Trunk and to be a member of this great family. I pledge my continued devotion and energies to this company and our future success. Together, I am sure we can make it happen."[4]

Categoric success in all areas remained predictably elusive. The Bandeen plan always had been to make GTC roads understood to be American carriers, not as Canadian National puppets. "I'm not sure we ever convinced the big shippers that we were independent, but we sure did everything we could to make sure that we would go to the shipper and say we are independent. We are a U.S. railroad and if you have a problem don't go to Canada with it 'cause they aren't going to help you. You have to come to us at Detroit. The only way we were going to get the respect of the shipper was to be faster on our feet and more responsive than the big railroads. So that was part of our arrangement, that we were to be very quick, very responsive, and react immediately. And we would take a very prominent position within the shipping group. Walter Cramer was a member of the National Freight Transportation Association. And I would be a director of the Association of American Railroads, President of the Michigan Traffic Association and so on."[5]

"I'm firmly convinced that the railroad is here for one purpose: The service of the customer. If we don't render service we have nothing to sell, we have reduced income and thus no opportunity to maintain our operation and our physical plants," argued the vigorous, plain-spoken Burdakin. "We have to be responsive to the shipper's needs. That means service as well as rates as well as equipment. But the shipper needs certain levels of service and it is absolutely imperative that you perform to that level. If you don't have a good roadbed to run your trains on, it's impossible to perform the service. If you can't perform the service, you will find that you don't have a freight car load, somebody else has that. So, a good roadbed is essential to the game plan of Grand Trunk." But it costs lots of money to have high-quality track. "Well, it does cost money, there's no question it costs money. But it was money that we would eventually save. Poor track structure results in mechanical problems. One pulls the other. The more low joints that a freight car goes over the more . . . nuts, bolts, rivets would get loose on it. I think it's necessary to have an actual, absolutely sound railroad underneath your train. It does require money. But I think . . . it winds up being cost-effective." That explained Burdakin's determination at Grand Trunk Western, as an example, to add twenty miles of continuous-welded rail every year (thirty-year cycle), 100,000 ties annually (thirty-five-year cycle) as well as expanded centralized traffic control and system-wide microwave capability. "We are proud of our physical property . . . and the improved maintenance level," Burdakin told CN's board in 1976. "We believe we have earned the reputation of the 'Good Track Road,' but it is a reputation that must be won every day over every mile of track."[6]

So, how did the Grand Trunk properties stack up in the tumultuous and in many ways frightening domestic railroad environment of the 1970s and against Bandeen's Americanization plan? Very well. Yes, there were setbacks as well as successes, and of future challenges there would be many. Yet GTW had trimmed its depressing annual losses to a tolerable level, and GTC's cash position had eliminated the drain by American properties on Canadian National. Reported Burdakin in 1976, "We have been able to generate the cash required for our capital programs and are now on the threshold of having excess cash." Not a bad report at all considering those traumatic days of the American railroad industry.[7]

Two vexing and interrelated issues continued to dog Burdakin's need, especially at GTW, to drive down the number of reportable injuries by encouraging safe operating practice and

Burdakin never missed an opportunity to advertise GTW as the "Good Track" road.

the need to get the story of Americanization of CN properties in the United States and the new style of management disseminated within the GTC family and out to the broad public. Burdakin always fully embraced the safety issue and was a passionate advocate, but the public relations matter was not one he had experience with, and he was not particularly comfortable with it. To his credit, he turned to a competent outsider, Tony Franco, who headed the largest and most influential public relations firm in Michigan. Franco proved an excellent choice because he was a master at handling external issues, getting Grand Trunk before the public, and putting together publication packages such as the GTC annual report. Franco's fingerprints were all over the *Presidential Express*—taking President Gerald R. Ford over GTW in Michigan from Flint to Niles, handled by a red-, white-, and blue-adorned Bicentennial locomotive 1776. It proved a marvelous chance to show off GTW and, at a personal level, an opportunity to meet and greet President and Mrs. Ford. The press was predictably giddy. As to the need for better internal communication, Burdakin saw the need but seemed slow to move on the matter. Eventually, however, was born *GT Reporter*, a newsletter that in time would win coveted awards as the best in the industry and, importantly, the best in the industry in generating understanding between labor and management. Burdakin understood the positive correlation between effective internal communication and safe practice, but as in so many cases, the "ship turned only a little at a time."[8]

In the case of *GT Reporter* it was a matter of success breeding success. Out of it came "focus groups" made up of managers and labor leaders including general chairmen of the various crafts. Each side had a "voice" articulated in a neutral setting; over time each side found it could be candid without anger; the result often was a combined campaign to prosper the company and its employees in an always trying competitive environment.[9]

Ups and downs continued along the way. Beginning in 1973, John Burdakin launched GTW on a path he hoped would turn the company into "a 21st century railroad in 1975." What he referred to was Automatic Car Identification (ACI), an electronic information system designed to locate and identify all of the company's freight cars and trains at a moment's notice—a plan that would provide the most comprehensive network in the North American railroad industry. The cost would be a staggering $7.5 million, but the system—said Howard M. Tischler, general manager of information systems—would provide a database of revenue statistics linked to car movements and thereby establish a reservoir of information for marketing and accounting purposes. Functionally, information would be gathered by trackside electronic scanners that "read" color-coded plates on rolling stock and locomotives and fed data to the company's new IBM Central Processor in Detroit. Wheel sensors would provide additional data from principal yards. Employment among clerks would be lowered through the reduction of car checking in the field and elimination of the punch card process. Tischler predicted a direct 11.32 percent return on investment over eighty-four months. Burdakin became a passionate advocate of ACI and preached its gospel to the entire industry.[10]

The Association of American Railroads took note of GTW's experiment with ACI and, in 1975, initiated intensive assessment of the concept. A buoyant Burdakin pointed out that the company was receiving 99.9 percent accurate data from its label scanner-wheel sensor-computer system. This resulted in the reduction of mishandled cars, cars delayed by lack of proper paperwork, errors in car movements, and per diem payments. "We believe our system . . . clearly pioneers a way for other railroads," said Burdakin. The Association of American Railroads eventually mandated that all rail cars in the country be applied with bar-code plates but, after great expenditures were made, powerful forces in the industry complained

President Gerald R. Ford's *Presidential Express* in 1976 proved a marvelous means to show off GTW and for Burdakin to meet President and Mrs. Ford.

of imperfections and, rightly or wrongly, ACI as an industry standard perished late in 1977 before total results had been tabulated and without providing a substitute system. Burdakin shook his head in dismay. Ironically, the industry in the early 1990s would consider a similar program—Automatic Equipment Identification. It took nothing away from Burdakin to say that he simply was ahead of his time.[11]

Meanwhile, the American railroad industry continued to sort itself out. The dreary story of Penn Central predictably took center stage. Track conditions continued to deteriorate, service levels plummeted, and labor unrest in 1973 led to a strike. Investors talked of liquidation, and politicians discussed nationalization. Penn Central would not survive. But Penn Central's service area was characterized by densely populated districts and heavy industry requiring dependable railroad service. A reluctant Congress finally moved. Consolidated Rail Corporation was born on April 1, 1976. Before that, however, preliminary plans were formulated that boldly proclaimed that Conrail would not be a receptacle into which all lines of all Penn Central predecessors would be thrown. Rather, Conrail would be much slimmer—shorn of many branches and even many main lines. This would result in dislocation for some rail customers and restructuring for all railroads in a broad area from Chicago, St. Louis, and Detroit to Washington, New York, and Boston. How would GTC's railroads—especially Grand Trunk Western—respond? That was John Burdakin's responsibility.[12]

To properly discharge that duty, Burdakin concluded, GTC required eyes and ears in Washington—senses of a person who knew the industry as well as the workings of the federal government, a person who could monitor developments and make informed recommendations. In this, Burdakin had marvelously good fortune. Basil Cole, whose father had been an operating officer at Union Pacific, and who also had become a railroader—heading the law department at Pennsylvanian Railroad and then Penn Central—would be GTC's Washington emissary and eventually would be involved in important legal proceedings on its behalf.[13]

Burdakin and Cole recognized that Conrail's ultimate configuration would be the outcome of often conflicting and always powerful forces—local, regional, and national transportation needs, public and private requirements, and political considerations of all stripes. United States Railway Association (USRA) planners—"itinerant philosophers," Cole labeled them—might be relied on to carve out Conrail's core lines, but there was sure to be much more pulling and hauling. The East's large, healthy roads—Norfolk & Western (N&W) and Chessie System—would be principal players. Where did GTW fit it? Burdakin initially did not see the road expanding its service area by way of large strategic acquisition. Rather, he thought it could solidify its position in certain Michigan markets by selective acquisitions of Penn Central operations. Burdakin focused on Muskegon, Grand Rapids, Saginaw, Bay City, and Lansing, which, he said, did "not generate enough rail traffic to sustain three railroads" (GTW, Chessie, and Conrail). GTW's plan, then, was to campaign against Conrail presence above Detroit and Battle Creek and to convince USRA to divide Penn Central lines lying north of those cities between GTW and Chessie. The effort was directed at Michigan politicians and business leaders ("Grand Trunk is basically a Michigan railroad") and took on a David and Goliath tone ("Give Michigan's smaller railroads a chance to compete").[14]

The arena that GTC had evolved in was rapidly disappearing. Burdakin was nervous. "I don't have any misgivings about competing with an equal," Burdakin said at public hearings on USRA's final plan, "but I do have reservations about playing football in my undershorts against a fully equipped team supported by the federal government." Here was a double entendre. The reference, of course, was to Conrail and reflected Burdakin's concern as to GTW's

It took nothing away from John Burdakin to say that he simply was ahead of his time in the ACI matter.

ability to compete with that federally created and federally financed giant. It also reflected a larger concern: the ability to compete with Conrail and other increasingly powerful roads—N&W and Chessie. In the case of the Michigan lines, the most immediate issue, USRA eventually made available to GTW 118.5 Penn Central track miles in and about Bay City, Midland, and Saginaw, plus 32.5 track miles from Ann Arbor Railroad between Durand and Ashley through Owosso (over which GTW previously had trackage rights). GTW bought well ($1.458 million) and quickly authorized a three-year improvement program ($5 million). It was money well spent. By 1979, a 23 percent return on investment would be realized.[15]

Burdakin, Cole, and team found themselves in a circumstance faced by countless railroad managers of the past: GTC roads, especially GTW, had to expand its service area, as well as gain and hold friendly connections through additional gateways. This would not be accomplished by new construction, as had been the case a century earlier, but by line acquisitions—such as the purchase of the former Penn Central segments in Michigan—or on a grander scale by purchase or merger of entire companies. That prospect, though, would be awkward for GTC given its youth—not even ten years of age—and its delicate financial condition. Moreover, as always, there were considerations unique to GTC, such as its ownership by foreigners—the need to have permission from "headquarters," from Parliament, and ultimately from the Canadian people. Such constraints weighed heavily on GTC's ability to respond nimbly. Nevertheless, Burdakin had assembled a talented team, and Bandeen as usual, would dare to do. There was no reason to count out Canadian National's American roads as the merger movement evolved into the era of megamerger.

Detroit, Toledo, & Ironton Railroad.

Detroit, Toledo & Ironton offered an attractive north-south chute in and out of Detroit.

Events conspired to focus on an opportunity close at hand—Detroit, Toledo & Ironton Railroad (DT&I) with its north-south route configuration from Detroit through Flat Rock in Michigan and to Lima and Springfield and finally Ironton on the Ohio River. During the 1920s DT&I had been controlled by the hard-charging Henry Ford, whose huge River Rouge Plant was served by the road. In 1929, however, Ford became disenchanted with railroading and sold DT&I to Pennroad Corporation, which heretofore had only a modest presence in traffic-rich Detroit. Eventually Pennroad sold DT&I to subsidiaries of Pennsylvania, which along with the parent, became parts of ill-starred Penn Central.[16]

DT&I's contribution to its owner's well-being thinned during the first half of the 1970s just as Penn Central's creditors sought recompense. Rumors circulated within the industry that Pennco would be willing to part with DT&I. Several carriers poked about and expressed interest in one way or another. Meanwhile, Pennco asked Salomon Brothers for a candid evaluation. The report was not encouraging. Salomon noted that DT&I's market share had slipped; that net profits per carload, coverage of interest and other fixed charges, and cash flow all had declined; and that the operating ratio had risen. Salomon attributed these problems to several factors: "a few large accounts" that comprised

DT&I's traffic base, Penn Central's collapse, and the collateral rise of other "neighboring and affiliated roads" had taken their toll. DT&I's costs had accelerated more rapidly than revenues, and it had a restricted route structure. Worst of all, warned Salomon, DT&I could not "expect to refund bonds maturing in March 1976 using traditional external sources of capital.[17]

At the same time, Norfolk & Western Railway analysts quietly scrutinized DT&I. They liked its potential and earnestly urged senior management to acquire the road, but N&W's top brass did not react as the company's analysts had urged. Meanwhile, USRA plans were

implemented on April 1, 1976, with the birth of Conrail. At the same time DT&I established regular through service to Cincinnati and established direct connections with GTW in Detroit (bypassing the Detroit Terminal Railroad). In addition, DT&I's urgent need to satisfy bond requirements was met through the sale of impressive landholdings and leaseback of equipment. But problems remained. Maintenance was trimmed and derailments were costly and damaged the road's credibility. Ford suffered a strike costing huge chunks of traffic, and Mother Nature played nasty and expensive tricks. Harsh cost controls were imposed during the fall of 1976.[18]

Pennco was increasingly restless. Did DT&I fit into Pennco—an organization that essentially oversaw Penn Central's nonrail assets? The answer, in short, was no. A railroad, Pennco concluded, was at best a headache. The issue for Pennco then became how to maximize the value of the property. To address that issue and to make DT&I attractive for suitors, Pennco brought in Robert A. Sharp as president. Sharp made personal contact with major shippers and labor organizations, delegated managerial decisions, and promoted an aggressive marketing

DT&I was in play. Who would be the winner?

campaign. With Cincinnati service firmly in place, Sharp urged solicitation for the maximum haul. This included vigorous attempts to lure traffic from central Michigan, GTW country, toward which John Burdakin showed little affection.[19]

In any event, early in 1977 Burdakin asked Bandeen for permission to investigate acquisition of DT&I. Bandeen predictably responded in the affirmative but pointedly told Burdakin that it "would have to be achieved without CN cash support" because "the parent company cannot be seen to be investing in additional U.S. rail plant at a time when our capital demands in Canada exceed our ability to finance internally." Bandeen recognized the potential for moving heavy traffic onto DT&I through Cincinnati, but he also saw another advantage in acquiring the road. This might be, he pointed out, "the means by which we obtain external equity participation in GTC, or GTW, through a private sale rather than a public sale of stock." Burdakin had a mandate. With Basil Cole, he met with Frank Loy, president of Pennco, and Jervis Langdon, former president of Penn Central and Pennco adviser. Burdakin knew that others—Southern, Louisville & Nashville, Chessie, and N&W—had expressed interest, but was surprised to learn that Langdon believed DT&I should be sold to a "group of railroads rather than one individual railroad." Failing that, however, Pennco would "issue a prospectus and solicit bids." Pennco promised to make traffic and financial data available but then stonewalled Burdakin's persistent requests. The reason became abundantly apparent on May 31, 1977, when Norfolk & Western and Chessie announced an agreement to jointly purchase DT&I for $15 million. Southern countered with an offer of more than $22 million, but on June 13 Pennco signed a binding agreement with N&W and Chessie (technically N&W and Baltimore & Ohio, a unit of Chessie) for $23.6 million. GTW had been frozen out.[20]

How to respond? Burdakin felt he had two options: negotiate a deal with the new owners to protect GTW interests or oppose the transfer of ownership before the Interstate Commerce Commission. Burdakin chose the latter. But he felt GTW's chances with the ICC would be materially improved if he could provide a realistic alternative to N&W and Chessie's proposal. A project team was assembled, headed by Basil Cole and Robert A. Walker, who was borrowed from Walter Cramer's marketing staff.

When N&W and Chessie made formal application to the ICC in the fall, GTW denounced the plan because of the "serious impact this sale could have on the competitive position and solvency of smaller roads—especially GTW." Indeed, said Burdakin, Grand Trunk Western was "completely dependent on the economy of Michigan" and this sale would "adversely affect the quality of service we render to the automobile industry and others." Basil Cole was much more direct. "This was a stab in the heart of Grand Trunk Western because Chessie and Norfolk & Western were both competitors of Grand Trunk and if they had DT&I under their control they would be in position to squeeze Grand Trunk out of much business . . . and do it fatal harm." Moreover, there was the important matter of fairness. Selling DT&I to two of the largest revenue-producing railroads was "not equitable." The campaign mirrored earlier efforts to gain USRA concessions—a David and Goliath contest certain to harm David and his worthy constituents if hardhearted Goliath had his way. Burdakin turned up the heat. Sale of DT&I to N&W and Chessie would have "monopolistic impact" that would clearly have negative impact "for smaller roads, shippers, communities, and taxpayers." GTW, he affirmed, would offer an alternative proposal. After all, "Detroit, Toledo & Ironton and Grand Trunk Western, Michigan-based railroads, have traditionally performed complimentary services especially in the highly industrialized southeastern section of the state."[21]

On February 16 GTW and GTC boldly asked the ICC to disapprove the N&W/Chessie application and indicate, on an interim basis, conditions by which it would approve control by Grand Trunk Western of DT&I *and* the Detroit and Toledo Shore Line Railroad (D&TSL or Shore Line, presently owned in halves by GTW and N&W). The purpose of this, said Cole, would be to integrate GTW, DT&I, and Shore Line into an efficient unit that would provide competitive balance and produce greater return than any or all of the three roads operated independently. Financing had been arranged by which GTW would issue senior unsecured notes guaranteed by GTC adequate to pay for DT&I stock and debt, land held by a subsidiary, N&W's half of the Shore Line, labor protection, and start-up costs. All of it was consistent with the Interstate Commerce Commission Act (to improve adequacy of transportation service), the Regional Rail Reorganization Act of 1973 (continuation and improvement of essential rail service), and the Railroad Revitalization and Regulatory Reform Act of 1976 (4Rs Act, restructuring of the system on a more economically justified basis and fostering competition among all carriers). Cole asserted that DT&I and GTW were "natural candidates" because their combination would result in an end-to-end merger. GTW pledged that these efforts were not, as N&W and Chessie charged, designed simply to derail its application. GTW would pay $15 million for DT&I stock, but was flexible in that regard if Pennco could demonstrate greater value.[22]

This campaign, Basil Cole readily admitted, would be "an uphill battle." Innovation and persistence would be required. It was incumbent on GTW to present itself as "the little guy" battling the "giants" or the basis of "everlasting right." Privately, Cole told Burdakin that N&W and Chessie had the best argument. Burdakin bluntly responded that if they succeeded, it "would kill GTW as well as DT&I." GTW purposes were at once, Robert Walker urged, strategically offensive (get to Cincinnati and connections there) and strategically defensive (prevent any encroachment of Detroit's traffic base). GTW designs might be aided by altered public opinion; the broad issue of railroad mergers certainly was not as explosive as it once was. In fact the Railroad Revitalization and Regulatory Reform Act of 1976, passed ostensibly to address growing crises in the Midwest, actually enhanced opportunities for merger and rationalization of plant. Cole's burden as counsel would be to convince ICC staffers, the administrative law judge hearing the case, and ultimately the commissioners themselves that the GTW plan was better than that of N&W and Chessie in terms of "public interest."[23]

Big guns were arrayed against GTW/GTC. Pennco, owner of DT&I, was put off by the fact that Grand Trunk had interrupted what seemed to be a fait accompli, that GTW—unlike N&W and Chessie—had not negotiated a sales contract, and had not even made a solid dollar-value offer, and it clearly doubted Grand Trunk's ability to finance the deal. After all, said Pennco, GTW has a "history of serious financial difficulty." And, sniffed Pennco attorneys, GTW's "bifurcated proceeding" was altogether "inappropriate."[24]

Opposing attorneys also took great issue with Grand Trunk Western's vaunted claims to recent success under the flag of Grand Trunk Corporation. There were, in fact, said N&W and Chessie, "sharp limits to the degree of [GTC's] 'independence and Americanization.'"[25]

What were Canadian National's intentions in the DT&I case? "CN is not seeking to expand its operations within the United States and is not even committed to maintaining full ownership of its American rail subsidiaries," said counsel. In other words, CN's interest in the DT&I case was a matter of enhancing the attractiveness of its U.S. investments rather than simply expanding the CN system. Success in this case by N&W and Chessie would damage GTW, whereas a combined GTW-DT&I-D&TSL would "make outside investment in GTW more attractive." This was, of course, Bandeen's long-term desire, and he had told Burdakin as much in 1977: "My main reaction . . . is in seeing this proposal as a possible means by which we can obtain external equity participation in GTC, or GTW."[26]

The whole matter of Canadian National—a "foreign corporation"—and its relationship to GTC and GTW was admittedly confusing and thus presented opportunities for opposing attorneys and others to fan xenophobic flames. Was there not something untoward about a "Crown Corporation," all of whose stock is owned by the Canadian government, doing business in the United States? Yes, implied N&W and Chessie, and yes, said Canadian Pacific (CP), CN's nemesis at home. This irked John Burdakin, who scorned those who contended that "Grand Trunk's acquisition of Ironton [DT&I] poses some sort of sinister threat to the United States by increasing Canadian investment in our U.S. railroad system." For his part, Bandeen found such assertions contradictory and bemusing. He noted that CN and CP were head-to-head competitors in Canada, where they fell under the same regulatory framework, and he pointed out that both had substantial investment in U.S. rail operations (CN through GTC and CP through Soo Line). "Consequently, I am," Bandeen chuckled, "at a loss to understand why Canadian Pacific . . . has endeavored to paint a sinister picture in describing the modest investment of CN in United States enterprises." What of Norfolk & Western and Chessie? Each had lines in Ontario, Bandeen reminded, "where they themselves compete with Canadian roads in Canadian territory." For GTW, the Canadian-ownership issue remained nettlesome but not controlling.[27]

The Detroit, Toledo & Ironton case seemed a microcosm of the industry at the time. Tremendous flux reflected a growing recognition that change had come and that the industry needed to make significant and appropriate adaptations. Merger was a continuing nostrum, but by most standards of the day the DT&I matter was small potatoes. In the Midwest and West, Milwaukee Road ended service west of Miles City, Montana, early in 1980 and on March 31 of that year Rock Island simply died. Line abandonments and redefinition of service area would continue in those regions as a consequence. Unrelated to the problems of Milwaukee and Rock Island but of great consequence otherwise was the merger of St. Louis–San Francisco (Frisco) into the already huge Burlington Northern empire—also in 1980. Big news also came from the East. Late in 1978, Chessie System announced negotiations with Seaboard Coast Line Industries that would result two years later in creation of CSX, a holding company for Chessie (Chesapeake & Ohio, Baltimore & Ohio, Western Maryland, etc.) and Seaboard (Seaboard Coast Line, Louisville & Nashville, etc.). Not surprisingly, Norfolk & Western and Southern then announced study plans that on June 1, 1982, would result in formation of Norfolk Southern.[28]

All of this was bound to have heavy impact on all of the GTC roads in one way or another. There were direct and indirect reflections in the DT&I case. For instance, the Burlington Northern–Frisco merger mirrored ICC's then-current affection for end-to-end combinations. In addition, the demise of Rock Island and bankruptcy and massive line abandonment by Milwaukee—following as it did the crisis of eastern lines leading to painful loss of rail service and then creation of Conrail—made the public, politicians, and the ICC unwilling participants in further railroad misery. Thus GTW's contention that the Shore Line and maybe even itself were headed for the poorhouse hit a responsive nerve. The David and Goliath routine worked. So did Cole's legal strategy. On July 30, 1979, the ICC administrative law judge who heard the case ruled that both applications (GTW's and that of N&W/Chessie) met public interest requirements, but he expressed preference for GTW. A formal decision would follow.[29]

A flurry of activity unfolded—appeals, negotiations, pulling and hauling of all types. Most interesting, perhaps, was the campaign of Robert Sharp and others in DT&I management who, with investors and Cincinnati businessmen, attempted to form a group to acquire DT&I. Sharp's proposal had appeal since the arrangement would not be subject to ICC authority and thus the consortium could undertake a direct sales arrangement with Pennco. As it turned out, Pennco was negotiating with several other parties. Meanwhile, Norfolk & Western, Canadian Pacific, and others petitioned the ICC for review. Events moved quickly to resolution. GTW's board on March 19, 1990, authorized Burdakin to bid (not more than $33 million) for the outstanding stock of DT&I. On April 1, Pennco agreed to an aggregate price of $25.2 million, and on June 18 the Interstate Commerce Commission gave its blessing. The Detroit, Toledo & Ironton Railway had a new shareholder, Grand Trunk Western Railroad, and a new president—John H. Burdakin.[30]

The ICC appended a most important sidebar. Grand Trunk Western was required either to purchase the remaining one-half interest in the Detroit & Toledo Shore Line from Norfolk & Western or to divest its own interest. Stung by its defeat in the DT&I matter, N&W resolutely refused to sell its stake. This placed GTW in difficult straits, made more so by ICC's further requirement that full responsibility for the issue rested with GTW. Matters remained awkward, but when N&W sought merger with Southern, GTW finally found a chink in N&W's defense. GTW complained that a combination of these two companies would harm its welfare and, to smooth things, N&W grudgingly agreed to grant protective concessions via Cincinnati and to sell its interest in Shore Line. The agreed price was $1.9 million; GTW took full control on April 13, 1981. The Detroit & Toledo Shore Line Railroad was dissolved on September 30, 1981.[31]

With DT&I safely under its belt, GTW with CN and others developed
Montreal–Atlanta service via Port Huron and Detroit.

Chapter 7

Jilted

GRAND TRUNK CORPORATION'S SUCCESSFUL CAMPAIGN TO ACQUIRE DETROIT, TOLEDO & Ironton and Detroit & Toledo Shore Line during the late 1970s played out at a time when the railroad industry in the Midwest was undergoing wrenching change. Be it remembered that Chicago, Rock Island & Pacific (Rock Island)—"the mighty fine line" of musical verse— had declared bankruptcy in 1975 and tottered toward oblivion. The end came on March 31, 1980; it was the largest abandonment ever, 7,500 miles. Almost simultaneously Chicago, Milwaukee, St. Paul & Pacific Railroad (CMStP&P or Milwaukee Road), bankrupt since December 19, 1977, abandoned its Pacific Extension west of Miles City, Montana, as well as other trunk routes and various branches—paring down, its trustee said, to carry on as "Milwaukee II," a mere shadow of its former self and utterly without assurance of survival as a regional carrier or in any other form. In addition, neither Chicago & North Western (C&NW or North Western) nor Illinois Central Gulf could claim robust balance sheets at the time. Many observers gloomily concluded that the horrible "eastern bankrupts" malady now was abroad in the midlands. That raised the specter of government involvement with vast expense, à la Conrail, a specter not at all attractive to politicians or rail managers. Yet significant restructuring in the region was at hand, with or without government planning or financial involvement.[1]

Managers at both Grand Trunk and Canadian National watched it all with captivated interest. They recognized the need to adjust to changed circumstance, and they recognized that the flux created strategic threats but also strategic opportunities. Yet the DT&I and Shore Line cases had been long and taxing, and now John Burdakin and his colleagues were hard at the business of consolidation and integration. Burdakin and team pored over maps, exploring opportunities, but they acknowledged the immediate imperative— digesting the new acquisitions. Robert Bandeen cautioned Burdakin: The main objective for Grand Trunk Corporation was to protect Canadian National's interests. That *might* be accomplished by extending GTW's line haul through acquisition but, said Bandeen, ultimate benefits had to be clearly demonstrable. Moreover, Bandeen pointedly reminded, CN *might* best be served by selling off parts or even all of GTW. Yes, replied Burdakin, but making GTW more attractive to potential suitors *might* require extension into additional gateways offering new and attractive marketing opportunities. Such opportunities were more likely for smaller roads and regional carriers, noted Burdakin, than for huge railroads born of the megamerger movement. The small versus big or David and Goliath approach had succeeded nicely for GTW in recent forays. There was no reason to expect less in future endeavors. Bandeen agreed.

Burdakin's eye increasingly fell on Kansas City as a potential outpost. Connections could be made there to the Gulf Coast through independent regionals Kansas City Southern (KCS) and Missouri-Kansas-Texas; to Texas points via Burlington Northern; to Texas, the Southwest, and Southern California by way of Santa Fe and after early 1980 by Southern Pacific; and to the central West via Missouri Pacific, Union Pacific, and shortly Denver & Rio Grande Western. In this regard, Rock Island offered GTW twin alternatives from Chicago (Blue Island): via Des Moines to (1) Kansas City and (2) Omaha. GTW's strategic team, led by Robert Walker, was dismayed, however, by the wretched physical condition of Rock Island property.[2]

At the same time, however, CMStP&P continued to flounder in a sea of red ink. Initial plans for a "core" operation had not included Milwaukee's route from Chicago to Kansas City, although eventually it was retained. Given Milwaukee's severe cash shortage and the nervousness of politicians and government bureaucrats over the growing Midwestern rail crisis, Burdakin reasoned that GTW might gain access to Kansas City by purchasing its line. But there was more in the Milwaukee than just its Kansas City line, which attracted GTW managers who increasingly studied acquisition of much of that company's then-condensed route structure: Milwaukee would give GTW its coveted longer haul with an appendage to Kansas City; it would provide additional opportunities in and around Chicago; it would allow GTW to tap the traffic-rich city of Milwaukee; it would extend line haul advantages to and from the Northwest via St. Paul / Minneapolis; and, more important, it would give GTW trackage rights between St. Paul and Duluth, a direct connection with Duluth, Winnipeg & Pacific, and in that way satisfy historical urgings to link GTW solidly with CN's western traffic base.

Milwaukee's struggle continued—indeed, there followed a gallant struggle for life. Huge segments of embargoed line were sold—764 miles in South Dakota alone—to bring in cash. Scrap from abandoned lines and excess equipment produced further infusions. Track supplies rendered surplus were quickly installed to bolster surviving lines, and rolling stock was patched and painted. Employees, at least most of them, agreed to "wage deferrals." Observers detected an aggressive new spirit. Perhaps Milwaukee would not follow Rock Island to the boneyard. The trustee, former Illinois governor Richard B. Ogilvie, and Worthington L. Smith, Milwaukee's president, focused on the road's primary routes: Duluth–Twin Cities–Milwaukee-Chicago; Chicago-Louisville; and, Chicago–Kansas City.[3]

On September 15, 1981, Ogilvie filed a revised plan of reorganization—one that predicted a financially viable, 2,900-mile "north-south regional railroad." The plan, said Ogilvie, anticipated profitability in 1983 and a 12.2 percent return on investment in 1986. The plan would also make the Milwaukee more attractive to other railroads, although Ogilvie said there were no acquisition discussions at the moment.[4]

No formal discussions at least. On June 23, 1980, John S. Guest of Lehman Brothers Kuhn Loeb told John Burdakin that Milwaukee "would be available for acquisition at some point in the future" and wondered if there was interest at Grand Trunk Corporation. "We are on the verge of digesting a rather full plate with DT&I," Burdakin had told Guest in reply, but, he added, "the subject has considerable interest to us." Considerable interest, indeed. On the same day Burdakin told Walter Cramer and Paul E. Tatro that "sometime in the near future we would discuss the merits of becoming involved."[5]

Sixteen months later, on October 27, 1981, GTC and Ogilvie announced that "discussions concerning the possible integration of the Milwaukee Road into the GTC system of

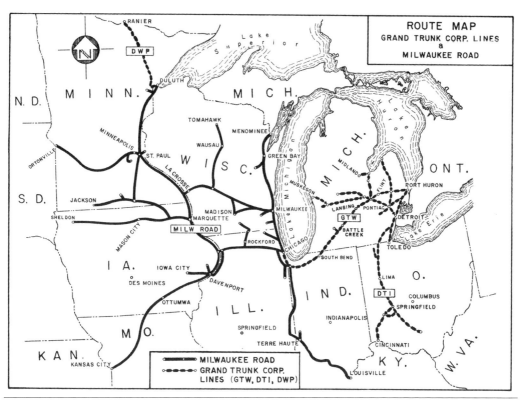

Combination of GTW/DW&P with Milwaukee Road would be a marvelous example of an end-to-end merger of the type favored by the Interstate Commerce Commission.

railroads" had begun. Rumors of GTC's interest had circulated since summer when GTW personnel toured Milwaukee properties and when Canadian National began routing increased volumes of lumber to CMStP&P at Duluth via DW&P.[6]

The strategic logic was obvious. The double-track Milwaukee main line between Chicago and St. Paul coupled with Milwaukee's trackage rights over Burlington Northern to Duluth would provide a direct high-speed, high-capacity means to link two disconnected properties—Grand Trunk Western and Duluth, Winnipeg & Pacific. The combination "would create a 5,000-mile system that practically would encircle the American side of the Great Lakes." More important, line hauls would be extended with commensurate increase in revenues. Milwaukee's Duluth–St. Paul–Chicago-Louisville leg would be of particular advantage to CN and DW&P for movements from western Canada, and the Chicago–Kansas City line would more than double GTW's haul on automobiles and parts. And the combined properties would boast an impressive traffic mix protecting revenues otherwise sensitive to the business cycle.[7]

GTC's move brought mixed comment. Speculators, who hoped Milwaukee would be liquidated in the fashion of Rock Island, were dismayed at the prospect of a reorganized Milwaukee and sale of it to GTC. Industry leaders, most of whom thought that even Milwaukee's core would be dismembered, were cautious in their early appraisal.   Most, it seemed, were surprised by GTC's aggressive new personality. Managers of Milwaukee's neighbors—Burlington Northern, Soo Line, and Chicago & North Western—had profoundly hoped for

Rumors of GTC's interest in CMStP&P mounted when Grand Trunk personnel toured Milwaukee's lines. Portage, Wisconsin, November 10, 1981. (John Gruber photograph.)

Milwaukee's liquidation and thus pondered this unexpected turn of events and wondered what impact an expanded GTC would have on their respective fortunes.[8]

John Burdakin's face lit up at the prospect of acquiring Milwaukee, but in predictable form he demanded only a dry-eyed assessment of Milwaukee's capacity. Robert A. Walker, Paul Tatro, and Basil Cole, the nucleus of the GTC team, found that a difficult assignment.[9]

By mid-February 1982, Walker and the others prepared internal documents that proposed reallocation of traffic from Canadian National, DW&P, and GTW adequate to "bring Milwaukee II sufficient revenue to lift it from bankruptcy, make it profitable, and enable it to return cash to its owner." These were bold words from staffers who frankly remained unconvinced but who understood Burdakin's increasingly positive position on the question. The arrangement they proposed would amount to perhaps eighty thousand cars per year and would, they hoped, move Milwaukee from the category of pretax loss to net income. Burdakin headed for Montreal and a meeting with Bandeen. Both men agreed: Milwaukee was worth pursuing, for it had potential to benefit parent and children as well.[10]

On May 24, 1982, John Burdakin and Richard Ogilvie jointly announced that they had signed a letter of intent providing for transfer of stock ownership in Milwaukee to Grand Trunk Corporation—but only after Milwaukee was reorganized. GTC agreed to shoulder $250 million of Milwaukee debt and obligations, but the estate, principally Chicago Milwaukee Corporation, would retain Milwaukee Land Company, a valuable subsidiary of the railroad. At the same time, GTC and Milwaukee agreed to immediate "operating initiatives" designed to increase traffic volumes and revenues to Milwaukee.[11]

On May 24, 1982, John Burdakin, right, Richard Ogilvie, center, and Worthington Smith, left, announced that a letter of intent had been signed by which GTC would acquire stock ownership of CMStP&P.

Burdakin invoked his best David and Goliath routine. Consolidation of Grand Trunk and Milwaukee was essential to survival "in an environment dominated by larger railroads that are growing even larger by the merger process." Government policy, Burdakin insisted, should encourage smaller railroads by giving them a chance to compete with industry giants. Failure to do so might result in further "emergency transfusions from the taxpayer to support tottering finances of bankrupt railroads." The proposal to consolidate GTC and Milwaukee would be "an opportunity for two relatively small end-to-end rail systems to gain strength through cooperative efforts while improving their service to the public." Indeed, GTC/Milwaukee would create strong competition in the Midwest with the Kansas City gateway as the focal point.[12]

A "marketing blitz" is what *Railway Age* called a six-week GTC/Milwaukee campaign ramrodded by Walter Cramer with the full cooperation of Peter C. White, head of Milwaukee's marketing group, to acquaint shippers with "unprecedented joint train operations" and other advantages offered as a part of what the roads jointly labeled their voluntary coordination agreement (VCA). These advantages often extended beyond the service territory of GTC/Milwaukee. For instance, Southern Pacific—which recently had acquired and upgraded Rock Island's portion of the Golden State Route west of Kansas City—joined with Grand Trunk Western, Canadian National, and Milwaukee to improve transit time on lading moving to and from Montreal and Toronto and Southern California via Port Huron, Chicago, and Kansas City. GTC and Milwaukee also engaged in an innovative and attractive advertising campaign pointing to "one great service from two great rail systems."[13]

Attention was diverted elsewhere to matters that, at first blush, seemed unrelated to GTC's efforts to acquire Milwaukee. In fact, there was a direct relationship to the realignment resulting from Milwaukee's departure from many markets coupled with the total collapse of Rock Island, on the one hand, and GTC's campaign to acquire Milwaukee's corpse, on the other. Particularly at issue was Rock Island's route between St. Paul and Kansas City—the "Spine Line," as many dubbed it—and Rock Island's impressive grain-gathering branches in Iowa. As early as 1979, Chicago & North Western had promoted a bold plan to take over Rock Island and Milwaukee lines in Iowa and southern Minnesota. Iowa authorities bridled at this

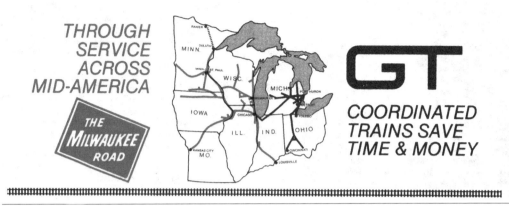

GTW and Milwaukee jointly mounted a "marketing blitz" to ballyhoo their voluntary coordination agreement.

notion, citing potential antitrust problems, and openly backed counterproposals by Kansas City Southern, whose new presence would encourage competition and prevent monopoly by C&NW. Milwaukee itself coveted the Spine Line, as did Burlington Northern, which even offhandedly proposed joint ownership of it with KCS to form a new operator, Kansas City Northern. Bidders haggled with Rock Island's stern trustee to no avail, and, when Rock Island went down for the count on March 31, 1980, the trustee gave C&NW only a short-term lease before the ICC designated North Western as operator of the Spine Line under directed service order.[14]

The VCA took graphic form as all participants—Canadian National, Duluth, Winnipeg & Pacific, Grand Trunk Western, and Milwaukee Road—pooled efforts and equipment designed to strengthen CMStP&P.

Matters became increasingly muddled when Soo Line entered the fray. Fresh from its recent acquisition of tiny Minneapolis, Northfield & Southern (MN&S), Soo Line—nearly 56 percent owned by CN's historic rival, Canadian Pacific—entered a bid on September 14. Acquisition of MN&S, incidentally, provided Soo a direct short-mile connection from the west side of Minneapolis to the Spine Line south of St. Paul at Northfield. Moreover, the Spine Line had clear strategic importance for Soo, traditionally a grain-handling road. But was that the whole cloth? Several observers considered Soo's activity simple retaliation, orchestrated by Canadian Pacific, in reaction to GTC's plan (read, in this case, Canadian National's plan) to acquire Milwaukee.[15]

Soo managers, for their part, found such speculation bemusing since Canadian Pacific took little notice of the entire matter. In fact, said Byron D. Olsen, vice president-law at Soo, "Our problem . . . was getting CP interested in what we wanted to do." Olsen and others at Soo were frightened, however, by C&NW's aggressive posture and urged a policy to build Soo "into a size that could better balance the main competition in its service region [C&NW]." But that process was halting. CP had little strategic interest in Soo at the time, and Soo itself had no culture of acquisition to speak of. Consequently Soo groped to define itself anew with little direction from its principal shareholder.[16]

The spotlight shifted to Chicago & North Western, whose president vociferously complained of what he called "the Canadian invasion," an obvious reference to Grand Trunk Corporation in pursuing Milwaukee and Soo's attempt to acquire the Spine Line and attendant branches. A bidding war ensued, and the Interstate Commerce Commission, at sixes and sevens, approved both bids; it would fall to Rock Island's trustee to make the decision.[17]

GTC and CN kept deliberately low profiles in the Spine Line case. Internally, however, the position was clear: C&NW was favored over Soo, since a decision favoring Soo would strengthen CP-Soo over CN-GTC-Milwaukee. CN's view was especially pointed because, of the many advantages Milwaukee offered, the greatest—insofar as CN was concerned— was the Duluth–St. Paul–Chicago route to which CN planned to route heavy traffic from western Canada if GTC acquired Milwaukee. In that same Duluth-Chicago corridor were, of course, C&NW and Soo Line, but more important to CN's calculations were historic CP/Soo linkages from western Canada to Chicago (CP to Portal, North Dakota, and/or Noyes, Minnesota, Soo beyond).[18]

The Rock Island trustee finally came down on C&NW's side. Trackage in the amount of 720 miles passed to C&NW on June 29, 1983, and North Western quickly made good on its promise of major rehabilitation. There was relief at GTC and especially at CN. Without good reason.[19]

The Spine Line case, as it developed, merely anticipated a much greater struggle with far greater stakes, that is, resolution of GTC's proposal to acquire Milwaukee. Menacing rumblings were heard from two camps. Soo's chairman, Thomas M. Beckley, told his shareholders following the Spine Line decision that Soo was "reviewing alternative arrangements which might be made to secure better access to the Kansas City gateway."

Another Soo official was more direct: "We may ask for operating rights . . . into Kansas City . . . over the bankrupt Milwaukee Road." More ominous mutterings came from C&NW's James R. Wolfe, who energetically propounded the "Canadian invasion" theme. "I'm not too anxious to compete in a capital formation contest with the Canadian government," said Wolfe in direct reference to the "government-owned Canadian National Railway." Particularly galling to some was a provision of law forgiving certain debts owed the federal government in the event of Milwaukee's successful reorganization and subsequent acquisition by another carrier—at least if that carrier was owned by CN. That possibility seemed to some as an indirect subsidy to the government of Canada by American taxpayers.[20]

Earlier, in 1981, when Milwaukee was paring to its core, John Burdakin had canvassed numerous railroads with the idea that they severally acquire the Milwaukee core, put traffic on it, and operate the road as a joint facility. Burdakin was disgusted to learn that there was no support for the idea. Most saw Milwaukee as redundant, except perhaps for its Chicago-Milwaukee–St. Paul thoroughfare. There was, in fact, surprise that *any* carrier would be interested in it. "Ours was the only life preserver floating on the ocean," said Burdakin, and Ogilvie now exclaimed gleefully that a combined GTC/Milwaukee would be "a marriage made in heaven." And there was widespread support for it among shippers and politicians.[21]

Yet, as it developed, the voluntary coordination agreement, curiously proved all too successful. By putting traffic on Milwaukee two powerful points were made: (1) traffic diverted to Milwaukee from other carriers (from C&NW and Soo at Duluth, for example) had hurt those carriers, (2) Milwaukee Road was increasingly vibrant. Only then—after GTC's boldly innovative voluntary coordination agreement, rerouting business before the fact of combination, had most clearly demonstrated the great potential in a consolidated GTC-Milwaukee—was there criticism or protest. Now, however, yesterday's naysayers gathered to take a covetous look at the formerly cadaverous Milwaukee.

On March 31, 1983, Ogilvie presented an amended plan of reorganization to the federal court overseeing the case. The reorganized Milwaukee would "emerge from bankruptcy as an efficient organization, relieved of unprofitable lines, deficient equipment and facilities," and would become a subsidiary of Grand Trunk Corporation. Milwaukee's performance in 1982, said Ogilvie, "had proved its financial viability and the current plan," he continued, "satisfied various public interest criteria."[22]

The Interstate Commerce Commission, like the federal district court, had to rule on Milwaukee's reorganization plan and potential acquisition by others. It set July 27, 1983, as the deadline for bids. With only a few hours to spare, Chicago & North Western breathlessly delivered on its threat to file a contrary bid for Milwaukee. The ICC announced that it would consider C&NW's last-minute proposal, but Ogilvie denounced it. Then he hesitated. Then he hedged. His opposition was not unalterable. Ogilvie's waffling sent a profound shudder through the Detroit offices. Would all the work on this project be in vain? Had GTC enabled Milwaukee to prosper only to lose it?[23]

There was but a single common thread in the GTC and C&NW proposals: each wanted to acquire Milwaukee. GTC's plan, if approved, would link properties end to end: DW&P with Milwaukee at Duluth and GTW with Milwaukee at Chicago (by way of Indiana Harbor Belt, 49 percent owned by CMStP&P). Projected benefits would come from additional traffic tendered by each new partner to the other, not from consolidation; neither the GTC roads nor Milwaukee would experience substantial changes in modus operandi; no downgrading of service or abandonments were planned; no employees would lose their jobs as a result of the operating plan. And GTC roads combined with Milwaukee would encourage competition. C&NW's proposal, to the contrary, boldly proclaimed that too much competition remained in the service area of C&NW and Milwaukee and that combination of these two would have the very useful impact of reducing redundant service, trackage, and employee numbers. Approval of the C&NW plan would improve the position of a medium-sized American carrier, while approval of the GTC proposal would aid a foreign railroad and its owners (Canadian National and Canadian taxpayers).[24]

An intense public relations campaign followed. Labor understandably favored GTC's end-to-end plan, for it would yield employment stability, whereas C&NW openly admitted plans for line abandonments and job reduction. Governors of Minnesota, Wisconsin, and Iowa—states that made up Milwaukee's principal service area—sided with GTC.[25]

Some parties saw it otherwise. C&NW spokesmen picked at GTC's own Achilles' heel—GTW's historically poor financial performance and the relationship of GTC properties to CN and thus to the Canadian government. And what about the vaunted power of GTC's parent company? CN's Ronald E. Lawless, in defining the relationship of the parent to GTC was emphatic: the U.S. subsidiaries "would have to make it on their own . . . [and] . . . further develop traffic and pay dividends." He emphasized that they could not "depend on CN to finance deficit operations." That being the case, asserted C&NW, GTC was nothing but a "floundering enterprise" that would "perpetuate instability in the Midwestern rail system" if it gained Milwaukee. "The Midwest does not need a mini–Penn Central," C&NW concluded in a shrewd reference to the Penn Central debacle and the resulting expensive governmental involvement to stabilize the industry in the Northeast.[26]

The matter was about to become even more complicated. In the fall of 1993, Soo Line's chairman told his shareholders that Soo was "opposed to both proposals [GTC and C&NW] and continues to study possible alternatives to restructuring the Milwaukee Road." Soo announced on January 13, 1984, that it would file a motion with the bankruptcy court to buy Milwaukee with a cash payment of $40 million and assumption of debt. The powerful smell of cash had an immediate effect on Judge Thomas R. McMillen, who was overseeing the

High Stakes Poker or Who Will Save Public Interest?

The Milwaukee Road contest did, indeed, become a "high-stakes poker game."

proceedings and reopened the bidding. There was predictable distress at C&NW and utter dismay at GTC.[27]

Judge McMillen did indeed accept Soo's application, and a bidding war quickly erupted—reminiscent of that for Rock Island's Spine Line. GTC amended its position to permit the estate to retain tax benefits. Soo increased its cash offer to $148 million, and C&NW dropped its plans to abandon Milwaukee trackage. GTC's clearly was an inferior bid on a comparative basis, a disappointment to Ogilvie, who admitted that the voluntary coordination agreement with GTC roads had much to do with Milwaukee's improved fortunes and who seemed embarrassed at this turn of events. GTC portrayed the contest as a public-interest issue—with GTC wearing the "white hat," but with Soo Line, C&NW, and Chicago Milwaukee Corporation all wearing "black hats" as they played a game of high-stakes poker with the public welfare at stake. It was clever, but not effective. Cash bidding continued, but only with Soo and C&NW as contestants. GTC was reduced to complaining, "We had a deal" and to preaching the wisdom of forming joint operating agreements by which all applicants could be served. The ICC promised a decision by late summer.[28]

The regulatory agency had a very hot potato on its hands. The first order of business was to deal with GTC's request for dismissal of C&NW and Soo applications. The motion was summarily denied without comment; it was an ominous sign.[29]

The commissioners then turned to merit of the various proposals. GTC's bid received high marks for public benefits since it was an end-to-end proposition, C&NW's received low marks because it included or implied line abandonments, and Soo's was viewed as a mixture of rationalization and lengthened line haul. No plan would have a negative effect on energy and environment, but in terms of employment GTC ranked high, C&NW low, and Soo between. All were judged as financially acceptable, although commissioners concluded that C&NW's offer was best for shareholders and claimants. In the end, however, they could only agree to dismiss Grand Trunk Corporation as a contender. They could not agree between the remaining candidates, C&NW and Soo, but approved Soo's proposal and took no action on C&NW's request. A divided commission sent its report to the applicants and to the bankruptcy court on September 10.[30]

Disappointed GTC managers already had decided to drop out of the contest, which continued along its bizarre path. Bidding continued to escalate, as did a nasty verbal war between C&NW and Soo. Richard Ogilvie, who as trustee had long supported GTC's bid, now favored a $781 million offer of cash and debt assumption by C&NW over Soo's $571 million offer. Citing public-interest factors, however, Federal Judge McMillen surprised all hands—especially Soo Line—by accepting the lower bid. Thus Chicago, Milwaukee, St. Paul & Pacific Railroad became a Soo Line subsidiary at 11:58 P.M. on February 19, 1985.[31]

Why had John Burdakin's dream foundered? Why had the "marriage made in heaven" dissolved at the altar? Basil Cole, GTC's seasoned attorney, maintained that "GTC had the best public-interest argument," but close associate Robert P. vom Eigen, declared that "we were in town with the wrong argument—meaning that GTC had trumpeted the virtues of public interest, an approach that had served it well in the earlier DT&I case, while the prevailing mood in Washington subsequently had shifted. The Reagan administration presently placed full value on deregulation and marketplace solutions of the type put forward by C&NW and Soo, putting much less emphasis on public-interest arguments. Cole further observed that GTC's position had been to "buy the debt and pay nothing for the property." That was fine as long as Milwaukee was financially anemic and perceived generally as without competitive ability; it was not fine when Milwaukee displayed vigor and threatened to live on as a competitive thorn abroad the Midwest rail landscape. That prospect, of course, aroused other contenders—those that had hoped to pick at the Milwaukee carcass. Then there was the matter of timing. C&NW and Soo both were wrangling over the Spine Line and might have remained sufficiently off balance if the GTC/Milwaukee case had gone forward even a few weeks earlier. GTC legal maneuverings also had delayed proceedings so that C&NW and then Soo had time to gather their wits. C&NW attorneys sensed that GTC would lose if the contest became a bidding war, for they perceived that GTW was hard-pressed for requisite cash. They also perceived that Canadian National, standing always in the wings, was either unable or unwilling to take a monetary position in Milwaukee. Soo attorneys agreed: "We felt that if GTC had the courage of its convictions early on and moved faster, it could have easily concluded acquisition of Milwaukee before North Western got off the mark . . . I appreciate that the foot dragging may not have been GTC's; CN obviously had much to say," concluded Byron D. Olsen. Yes, said Basil Cole, "We knew if the auction began, GTC would lose." That is exactly what happened.[32]

There were other problems. GTC did not have deep pockets. And GTC's recent foray into the merger field had not yielded predicted positive returns; DT&I, sad to say, proved a depressing cash drain during the soft economy of the early 1980s.

Circumstances north of the border surely influenced GTC's course of action. As always, Canadian traditions and political realities were key variables. In this case, at least some Canadians thought it untoward for CN to consider acquisition of substantial rail operations in the United States (albeit through an American subsidiary) when at the same time CN was trying to unburden itself of certain lines and functions in Canada.

Finally, when Robert Bandeen left Canadian National in 1982, GTC lost an ardent friend as well as a powerful advocate for strategic growth. Bandeen's direct and forceful approach and his determination to be an engine of change certainly earned him well-deserved plaudits within and without CN. "If he felt this was the right thing to do, he'd go ahead," recalled an admiring John Burdakin. If that ruffled feathers in Parliament or elsewhere, so be it. "He would handle it at the time." But any agent of change also provokes enmity among those resistant to change. After nearly a decade of being in the saddle at Canadian National, he likely was bruised and just as likely disappointed that change had not come along as rapidly as he had hoped. And the complexion of the CN board of directors had changed and was changing, businessmen or those disposed to sympathize with modern business principles and practice increasingly replaced by less capable "bag carriers," as Burdakin labeled them. In any event, Bandeen was gone, off to put his powerful imprint on Crown Life, an insurance company that had grown stale; in three years' time Crown's profits would quadruple. Bandeen's replacement, J. Maurice LeClair, a physician, was a political appointee, and although talented enough in many ways, knew little about the railroad industry and frankly paled in comparison with Bandeen. The change in leadership at Montreal certainly would be reflected at Detroit. Thereafter support for GTC was lukewarm at best in Montreal, where many at CN and on its board viewed the Milwaukee deal as a cash transaction and not as an assumption of debt for rolling stock, mortgages, and the like. Indeed, LeClair bluntly inquired of John Burdakin: "Why do you want to buy a bankrupt railroad?" The very question was telling of LeClair's lack of understanding and strategic vision. To be sure, Detroit had been obliged to prosecute the Milwaukee opportunity against long odds.[33]

The David and Goliath strategy, used so successfully earlier, was ineffective in the Milwaukee instance. In the end, John Burdakin and all who worked so diligently on the case were left to shake their heads and mutter of things that might have been. "Yes," said an emphatic Burdakin, "Ogilvie was right: It was 'truly a marriage made in heaven.'" Or so it might have been. "We prettied up the girl and took her to the dance, but she went home with the other guy in his Chevrolet," said Burdakin with a wry but very disappointed smile.[34]

Chapter 8

Soldiering On

It was not in John Burdakin's character to cry over spilled milk, but defeats in the Automatic Car Identification matter and then the Milwaukee Road issue rankled him. Indeed, these irritating twin burrs would forever be lodged in Burdakin's psyche. In both cases he had enthusiastically embraced an innovative position. In both cases he was, in an important sense, ahead of his time. In both cases powerful forces over which he had no control rose up to bring on defeat. In both cases he had fought the good fight only to taste the bitterness of failure. Wrenching disappointment was predictable. But it could not and would not be controlling.

"Mr. Burdakin." He did not overtly insist on being addressed in that fashion, but his wishes in that regard were indelible and well understood within the general office building and out across the properties. Back in 1971, at the outset of the GTC experiment, Earl G. Fontaine, as Robert Bandeen's stand-in, was given the responsibility of introducing GTW's three new vice presidents—John Burdakin, Walter Cramer, and Donald Wooden. In private he asked each man how he wanted to be addressed. Cramer said "Walt," Wooden said "Don." Fontaine then approached Burdakin, telling him the preference of the other two. Burdakin wrinkled his brow, thought a moment, and said: "Introduce me as John Burdakin." "Mr. Burdakin" was a clear reflection of Burdakin's upbringing as well as the strict conventions of the military in which he had served and, of course, his time at Pennsylvania Railroad. That formality also was typical of the domestic business world at the time and writ large in the railroad industry.[1]

Formality likewise presented itself in Burdakin's wearing apparel at work—without exception white shirt and tie, dark colored two- or three-piece suit, shoes shined. That certainly sent a nonverbal message that he expected others to be "properly attired" on the job. This, too, reflected a prevailing pattern of the time. Image was important. Jean Burdakin asked Earl Fontaine to "work on" her husband "not to be so formal in his dress on the job." Fontaine did as he was asked, and Burdakin did, over time, "loosen up a bit."[2]

Burdakin worked from his office. Subordinates came to him; typically he did not go to them. "Managing by walking around" was not yet in vogue, and it certainly was not his style. He exuded an air of superiority, was formal and was something of a chauvinist, an old-style manager. He was not a politician, no wheeler-dealer. A few perceived him as cold, hard, and rigid—especially early in his time at GTC. But as time went on, Burdakin was clearly seen as "a solid guy" with "a common touch" and interested "in you and your family." "How is your wife? How is your son, your daughter?" These were typical and frequent questions from

Burdakin when he visited with employees at all levels. And it was not show. His questions mirrored real concern and interest. He tried to read people, to understand them, to empathize with them, to appreciate their contributions to the company. In this he was largely successful. As one admirer put it: "He related to everybody on the railroad; they wanted to work for him."[3]

"What are your responsibilities as a manager?" Burdakin asked rhetorically of his cadre of leaders at GTC and then of members of the American Railway Engineering Association, adding quickly: "What is your role as an individual?" He asked the same questions of himself and responded firmly to each group: "It should be to make the world a better place. To make the world a place for less suffering and for less burden on our fellow man." Burdakin was unapologetic in publicly asking these very direct and penetrating questions and in giving his own bare-boned viewpoints. Was this some kind of irritating "holier than thou" sermon? Was he some kind of "Holy Joe?" Labeled a "stern Presbyterian," Burdakin took exception, saying that that label implied that he was a "far right, dictatorial conservative—staunch, stuffy, my way is the only way. I don't believe that's a true description." Of course it was not a true bill, but Burdakin was, in fact, a stern Presbyterian in the very best sense of the term.[4]

Others, inside and outside the GTC properties, took the measure of Burdakin's outlook on life. "Basically positive," said Howard Tischler; "the glass is half full, not half empty." "A class act" was the view of Howard Nicholas. "A very positive man," said Veronica Cabble and James A. Brewer. Burdakin was "a professional, a teacher, and did not take himself too seriously," argued David DeBoer. "Positive, humane, and caring," echoed Virginia Czarnik. "Straightforward and direct," recalled Jim Krikau. "Upbeat, optimistic . . . well respected by his peers in the railroad industry," added John Barriger. "A very positive outlook on life that was catching and infectious to all of those close to him," noted Phil Larson. "Mr. Burdakin had a very positive outlook with high morals and ethics," Gene Shepard pointed out. "John is a straight arrow," declared William McKnight. "He was a capable and strong leader with personal integrity that spilled over to his expectation of others," added Gloria Combe. Indeed, *integrity* is the word most often heard in defining John Burdakin's character.[5]

"What are your responsibilities as a manager?" Burdakin asked of his staff. The answer, he believed, should be "to make the world a better place"—both on and off the job. And he wanted that question to stay alive among his managers.

Burdakin's view was that the first requirement of a manager was competence followed closely by a devotion to the work ethic, an allegiance to honesty, a willingness to improve performance, a commitment to responsibility, an ability to detect a problem coupled with an ability to solve a problem, a team player, and a talent for teaching (leading) subordinates. How did others evaluate Burdakin's own management style and practice? "His was an aggressive, no-nonsense approach," said Charles Hrdlicka. "A no-nonsense type of guy," added James Brewer in chorus. "He led by example," recalled Virginia Czarnik; "a very smart guy and a good teacher" was the opinion of David DeBoer; "very knowledgeable and a hands-on style (a great combination)," in James Hagen's view. According to Ronald L. Batory, Burdakin's management style and practice was "always clear, concise, and consistent." "John was an even-tempered railroad manager. He could, however, set his jaw and be quiet, then firmly corrective," recalled William McKnight. "He did not practice an imperious style." Yes, Robert vom Eigen noted, he was "old school in that he had an almost military bearing of formality about him and he had an ego, but it was not out of control. You could disagree with him without fear of reprisal." Gloria Combe added: "His management style was demanding but fair. Unlike the militaristic nature of the rail industry at large, he did not admonish low performance with profanity or rants." Gene Shepard appreciated the fact that Burdakin "set guidelines and goals, and as long as you obtained them, he let you manage." Howard Tischler's recollection was similar: "John's style was basically one of empowerment. He gave you a goal to accomplish and resources to do it. And he was a good cheerleader." Phil Larson added: "His style was to lead by example that displayed his intellect and class. He gave you parameters but let you run your own candy store." Marc Higginbotham admired Burdakin for stressing "accountability (your word is your bond) and attention to detail."[6]

Burdakin's particular strengths, it was generally agreed, included his devotion to fairness and honesty, avoidance of micromanaging, accessibility, "executive presence," willingness to form and utilize management committees, intellect, humility, focus, willingness to listen to new ideas and take on major initiatives, ability to empower subordinates, energy, and honesty. Most of all: his *integrity*.

Was he perfect? No, but his assets greatly exceeded his liabilities. There is a thin line between determination and stubbornness, and stubborn Burdakin could be. This took various dimensions and often was moxie and not stubbornness. His form was not to tell managers what to do on a routine basis, and there were some who did not function well or adequately without constant guidance. Burdakin was slow to replace them. He got out on the property often enough, but in the general office building he diligently "protected turf"—including his own. That, however, meant that he did not "pop in" to deal with his direct reports. That would have been, he considered, an invasion of another man's turf, but it often limited free flow of dialogue on important issues. His was a "Sloan style" (formal, top down) management typical of the period 1940–1970 soon seen as outmoded and replaced in most locales by a much more fluid style that Burdakin would not be comfortable in. And, curiously, one strength that worked against him was his trusting nature, expecting that everyone shared his values and not recognizing that there were some who merely pandered to him by telling him what they thought he wanted to hear. Still another strength, loyalty, could work to his disadvantage when he was tardy in identifying shortcomings in his direct reports. Indeed, loyalty to subordinates, in general a desirable trait, could be detrimental if persons protected did not pull their weight. Finally, while Burdakin had a marvelous working relationship with Robert A. Bandeen at Canadian National, he did not adequately cultivate open relationships with others of importance in a lower rank who would still be on the scene at Montreal after Bandeen departed. This would come back to haunt him during the LeClair era at CN.[7]

Management styles changed even as the railroad landscape changed. (Sam Breck photograph.)

The business environment by 1985 was even more ferociously competitive than earlier. As always, GTC was expected to protect the best interests of CN, and, as always, managers of GTC properties confronted the need to be nimble and creative.

The competitive environment had changed—and was continuing to change—in dramatic and unalterable ways, as the American and Canadian economies moved from basic production or manufacturing to service. Industries long dependent on railroads—iron and steel, ferroalloy and copper mining, stone and clay quarrying, forgings, and so on—declined, when lighter materials were substituted for heavier ones, and both countries became increasingly dependent on imports from Europe and Asia. The problems of the railroads in the United States were exacerbated when the already vigorous trucking industry was deregulated in the 1970s.[8]

Further changes on the traditional competitive landscape resulted from passage of the Staggers Act, signed into law in October 1980 by President Jimmy Carter. Carter recognized that the modal monopoly of railroads had long since passed, that most transportation in the United States was subject to competition, that nearly two-thirds of the nation's intercity freight now moved by means other than rail, that the rail system was shunned by the financial community with resulting capital malnourishment, and that nationalization of the railroads would be inordinately expensive and otherwise undesirable. The Staggers Act, although it stopped short of wholesale deregulation, nevertheless substantially eased the regulatory burden on railroads, and it provided significant changes in rate-making procedures, legalized contract rates, established new cost-accounting principles, and streamlined abandonment and merger standards, among other things.[9]

None of this occurred without difficulty. As the chief executive of one carrier said, "The industry was strong for the principle of deregulation, but weak on the practice." Competition, especially for contract business, proved unexpectedly keen. There were other problems. Single-line service, single-carrier control of transportation from origin to destination, always desirable from the carrier's point of view, became even more so as the result of Staggers. Previously, railroads had been protected from antitrust action in the making of joint rates, but under deregulation they had reason to worry about prosecution by the Justice Department when they sought to negotiate rates on point-to-point shipments. The easiest way to avoid such potential liability was, of course, to own the track from origin to destination—in other words, expand the system through line acquisition or merger. Short of this, and in an attempt to force shippers to accept, as much as possible, single-carrier service, the large railroads closed traditional gateways and raised rates via others.[10]

Competition was hardly restricted to that among railroad companies; most, in fact, was with other modes. Trucks, waterway operators, and pipelines had extracted devastating tolls on railroads. The Staggers Act, of course, significantly reduced artificial restrictions on the inherent efficiency of steel-wheel-on-steel-rail transport, but modal competition was not going to disappear simply because of progressive legislation. American railroads remained an asset-rich, cash-poor, high-labor-cost industry with clearly inadequate return on investment. Other than investment in property, the only immediate opportunity seemed to be further effort in the merger field.[11]

Rumors were rife; reality was not far behind. In the West in 1982, Union Pacific gathered in neighboring Missouri Pacific and Western Pacific to become what many observers called an "unstoppable monster," and Southern Pacific and Santa Fe talked confidently of marriage. Closer to home, and far more ominous as far as GTC roads were concerned, CSX corporation was formed in 1980 to acquire the assets of Chessie System Incorporated and Seaboard Coast Line Industries. Old rivals Southern Railway and Norfolk & Western then pledged their troth on June 1, 1982. Included in these two new giants were historic competitors of Grand Trunk Western—Chesapeake & Ohio and Norfolk & Western—each of which had obtained intraline access to southern and southeastern markets via Cincinnati—Chesapeake & Ohio with Louisville & Nashville and Norfolk & Western with Southern. All of this surely had a negative impact on the fortunes of Detroit, Toledo & Ironton—recently acquired, in large part, for the purpose of gaining traffic advantages for GTW and CN through Cincinnati. Elsewhere, Timothy Mellon, a wealthy nabob, acquired Maine Central in 1981, Boston & Maine in 1983, and Delaware & Hudson in 1984. Mellon combined these as parts of Guilford Transportation Industries, clearly a power to be reckoned with in New England. The impact of these acquisitions on Central Vermont was not immediately apparent.[12]

Then there was Conrail, birthed with the federal government as midwife and suckled with the milk of federal funds and beneficial legislation, but also a political conundrum. Contrail served the densely populated Northeast, historically a prime manufacturing region, but one that suffered wrenching dislocation as the American economy changed course. Conrail shuddered under these continuing changes, under onerous labor requirements, under vicissitudes of extremely harsh winters, and under the simple pain of birth and early life. Many leaders in manufacturing, transportation, and government doubted its success and, in fact, freely predicted its demise. Policy planners in the Reagan administration found Conrail an acute embarrassment, an awful contradiction to their firm devotion to marketplace solutions. Not surprisingly, the Northeast Rail Services Act of 1981 permitted Conrail to stop functioning as an instrument of social policy and—like all other carriers under the Staggers Act—to respond to traditional business needs and challenges. This unshackling gave heart to an invigorated management team; shippers soon reported improved performance. Politicians remained impatient. Secretary of Transportation Elizabeth Dole announced that bids would be received for the property, but she was disappointed when the only early interest came from Conrail employees. Then, in the summer of 1984, surfaced several offers with varying caveats and conditions. CSX, for example, proposed a split-up of Conrail; Norfolk Southern (NS), on the other hand, proposed outright acquisition.[13]

Grand Trunk Corporation was busy with the Milwaukee Road case as the Conrail story unfolded, but the ramifications were clear enough to John Burdakin, who viewed an energized Conrail as a great threat to GTC's Grand Trunk Western and predicted dire consequences if either CSX or Norfolk Southern gained parts or all of Conrail. Burdakin was especially concerned with Norfolk Southern, which, he told GTW directors, if successful in its attempt to purchase Conrail "would be positioned to inflict serious financial pain." In testimony before a congressional committee, Burdakin said that a merger of Conrail and NS would alter traffic patterns, threaten the existence of small railroads, and destroy rail competition in the upper Midwest. Specifically, the merger would cost GTW 68,000 revenue carloads per year, force GTW to reduce its employment by 15 percent, and threaten the company's ability to remain competitive. "The public interest and the National Transportation Policy as most recently defined by the Staggers Act" and "the competitive impact" were issues of profound consequence in the Conrail case, Burdakin told Senator Donald W. Riegel (D-Michigan).[14]

"Grit your teeth and go after it" often was a motto employed by John Burdakin when a sense of determination was necessary. That was the case when the Department of Transportation supported Norfolk Southern's application—"a transaction," he thundered, promoted by the "U.S. government . . . that threatened GTW with insolvency." John H. Riley, head

As always, there were challenges. And, as always, Burdakin would "plow ahead."

of the Federal Railroad Administration (FRA), asserted that Norfolk Southern would make concessions to salve GTW's wounds, but Burdakin testily responded: "To date NS has offered nothing that would permit GTW to survive and remain a competitive force within the market it serves." Burdakin accused Riley's agency of misrepresentation.[15]

GTC managers recognized that a defensive posture alone was inadequate. They must do more than complain; a positive alternative was required. To that end, Robert Walker, with a nod from Burdakin, unveiled "Prorail," a system that would include GTW, Pittsburgh & Lake Erie (P&LE), and lines redundant to Conrail or made redundant by a Conrail/NS merger. Prorail would reach from Buffalo and Pittsburgh in the east to St. Louis and Chicago in the west. Among advantages to GTW and P&LE were added gateways and extended line hauls; the shipping public would benefit by preservation of at least a degree of competition in the heartland. Furthermore, Prorail would obviate most antitrust problems in a Conrail/NS combination.[16]

The dogged and dogmatic determination of Secretary Dole and FRA's Riley in support of Norfolk Southern eventually aroused the ire of Representative John Dingell (D-Michigan), chairman of the House Energy and Commerce Committee, which had jurisdiction over legislation necessary to consummate the sale. Dingell became increasingly suspicious that a combined Conrail/NS would substantially reduce competition and harm regional roads. Momentum finally shifted. In 1985, Burdakin told a congressional panel that a premier alternative to acquisition and merger was a public offering plan. Jervis Langdon Jr., who had been president and then trustee of ill-fated Penn Central, saw the matter similarly. So did many others. In the end, the federal government on March 26, 1987, sold its ownership interest in Conrail—the largest initial public offering in the nation's history to that point. The immediate challenge—merger of Conrail and Norfolk Southern—had been thwarted, and GTC's Prorail plan perished accordingly. In the long term, though, GTW still was confronted with CSX, Norfolk Southern, and Conrail—powerful rail competition throughout its service area. Such powerful rail competition simply added to the greatest competition of all—trucks.[17]

Collaterally with the Conrail case Burdakin ordered a vigorous campaign to reopen gateways closed by Conrail in 1981. That Conrail policy had precipitated a howl of protests from shippers and connecting carriers. GTW managers saw the action as "a midnight raid to steal traffic." Midnight or not, Conrail had made policy designed to win for itself maximum haulage. With gateways closed and optional routings voided, Conrail instituted single-line rates over its own routes that did little, if anything, to reduce shipper costs but required shippers, in many cases, to deal with it in a captive way. "For smaller lines living in the same neighborhood with Conrail is like being in bed with an elephant. Every move the critter makes is bound to make you nervous," said Burdakin with undisguised concern.[18]

Indeed, Burdakin was not a bit amused; he set his jaw and would not be a patsy. In addition to the very important economic issue, a profound principle was at stake: integrity. After all, Burdakin himself had affixed his signature to an agreement of December 18, 1975, that obliged GTW and Conrail "to each other in respect to rates, divisions, and through routes via existing junctions and gateways." A deal was a deal. Your word was your bond. Conrail had abrogated the deal, but no retaliation was permissible. Burdakin reminded senior managers that the agreement was binding on both parties: "Our belief that they have violated the agreement does not permit GTW/DTI to violate the agreement in fact, principle, or intent." The matter had broad implications. Giant railroads already controlled the bulk of traffic, and Burdakin felt compelled to ask: "Is it sensible to reduce rail competition further by wholesale elimination of competitive joint rates and routes?" Had it been the intent of the Staggers Act to ensure the *absence* of competition among railroads? "If allowed to go unchecked," Burdakin told a Senate subcommittee, "current trends will foster a non-competitive system of giant railroads, each dominant in a section of the country and facing no meaningful rail competition." It was David and Goliath reborn.[19]

The issue headed for the courts. Early results were mixed. A preliminary injunction went against Conrail, Conrail sued Grand Trunk, and Grand Trunk sued Conrail. Burdakin was adamant that the company see the issue through to resolution. GTW charged violation of the 1975 contract and that Conrail had, on a premeditated basis, closed gateways and routings for the purpose of monopolizing traffic. Finally, on April 18, 1986, a settlement was reached; Grand Trunk won injunctive relief and compensatory damages, but exact terms were sealed by the court. In an important related development, Conrail lost a crucial gateway routings case before the Interstate Commerce Commission with the result that shippers and carriers could seek restoration of routes closed earlier by Conrail. A GTW attorney who had orchestrated the case gleefully concluded: "Goliath 0, David 2." James Hagen, then at Conrail, admitted that his railroad "was very aggressive in using the new law to our advantage. John felt that we had disadvantaged GT and took us on in court and won some major concessions. While he and I disagreed it was never personal."[20]

These were no small victories. The war continued, however, and Grand Trunk Western remained a small regional carrier confronted on the east and south and throughout its service area by powerful rail competitors—Conrail, CSX, and NS—and thwarted beyond Chicago by failure in the Milwaukee case. Yet GTW had arrows in its quiver that, if cleverly employed, could give the road much needed leverage. There was no disputing the fact that GTW originated and terminated large chunks of traffic and that it acted as an important conduit for business moving to and from Canada. And the voluntary coordination experiment with Milwaukee had proved how impressive that innovative marketing device could be once thoroughly and enthusiastically embraced. Eyebrows had been raised at other carriers and at ICC when the arrangement had gone into effect, but in the mid-1980s the ICC and most railroads viewed the VCA concept as an appropriate procompetitive, intercorporation approach. A VCA, in fact, could be consummated without ICC approval and the interminable delay and expense of such proceedings.[21]

GTC managers had predictably looked for options should the Milwaukee case be lost. The development of a post-Milwaukee strategy was vigorously pursued by Robert A. Walker, who previously had held traffic-related discussions with Burlington Northern (BN) which had lines throughout the Midwest to the Texas Gulf Coast and to Puget Sound, and BN had a stable traffic mix and the ability to directly tap the markets of Dallas / Fort Worth, Denver, Memphis, and Birmingham, not to mention Seattle and Portland. A VCA with BN would provide a link between GTW and DW&P, would expand the traffic base and market mix of GTC roads, and would be compatible with GTC's goal of long-term profitability as Canadian National's arm in the United States. On August 21, 1984, directors of GTC approved cancellation of the Milwaukee VCA and institution of a more expansive VCA with Burlington Northern effective January 2, 1985. The new agreement provided for coordinated marketing and operations among GTC roads, Burlington Northern, and Canadian National over a 63,000-mile network in Canada and the United States. One part of the arrangement pertained to carload business routed via Duluth and Chicago, and the second related to intermodal traffic through the same gateways. The new agreement with BN was successful, and the concept had caught on and was embraced by many other carriers as they sought access to new markets, sought to increase equipment utilization, and sought to streamline intercarrier pricing. BN, for example, had six VCAs in place in 1989. Shippers applauded. This kind of cooperation "would have been out of the question" only a few years earlier, said a representative of the Ford Motor Company, "because railroads were totally territorial."[22]

Although John Burdakin longed to control events that affected the GTC properties, he found this an extremely elusive goal; especially in the transportation industry did managers find themselves subject to buffeting by gyrations in the national and international economies. So it was during the early 1980s, which proved particularly vexing for those of GTC persuasion. Anticipating low billings in 1981, Burdakin ordered reductions in capital accounts, which turned out to be a prudent decision. Recovery would not come until mid-decade, and the recession pasted the Midwest, "home to most of our rail lines," with a vengeance. Unemployment in Michigan hit a frightening 17.9 percent, and on GTC roads manpower was reduced by 9.3 percent in 1982 alone. Train operations were trimmed modestly, but this was a delicate matter considering the firm demands of shippers, particularly on GTW. The crunch came in 1983, when GTC was forced to borrow $20 million from parent Canadian National, a fact that thoroughly alarmed the parent. "We are positioning Grand

A new VCA with Burlington Northern began on January 2, 1985. Heavy tonnage behind combined power of CN, BN, GTW, and DW&P dropped down the sharp escarpment toward Duluth shortly thereafter.

Trunk for the future," said Burdakin. The process, he willingly admitted, would be "difficult and not without sacrifice." Moreover, he forthrightly continued, "I do not see any lessening of competitive pressures that all of us face in operating the company." Neither, however, did he see "any lack of confidence in achieving our goals." A stiff upper lip. "Do your best and work hard," he might have said.[23]

Part of the problem, ironically and disappointingly, was purchase of Detroit, Toledo & Ironton, which came into the GTW family almost simultaneously with the onset of the recession. DT&I, of course, like GTW, was tied in large measure to the fortunes of the automobile industry, which was down by the heels during the early 1980s. At the same time, DT&I's route structure and historic traffic patterns were substantially attacked as Conrail closed gateways and otherwise flexed its muscles, and as the prized Cincinnati gateway lost allure when friendly Louisville & Nashville combined with unfriendly Chessie and when friendly Southern joined unfriendly Norfolk & Western. All of it, warned Burdakin late in 1980, "bore ominous warnings for the GTW-DT&I future." Despite innovations such as *Thunderbolt*, new through train service between Port Huron and Atlanta (via Southern at Cincinnati), DT&I operating statistics reflected slack revenues and high expenses, the cumulative result of the recession and unanticipated competitive forces. DT&I's operating ratio leapt to 121.3 in 1982. Burdakin, perhaps recalling the horrific problems in merging Pennsylvania and New York Central, had promised a slow process in joining DT&I with GTC properties, but during the summer of 1983 plans accelerated to "simplify the corporate structure" by merging DT&I into GTW. Much had been done already to combine operations and marketing, so there was

To John Burdakin fell the distasteful task of eliminating jobs during the recession of the early 1980s. Important shop forces would not be immune. (Sam Breck photograph.)

little notice on December 31, 1983, when the proud Detroit, Toledo & Ironton Railroad Company passed from the scene to be fully integrated by GTW.[24]

Burdakin's forces constantly looked for means to wean GTW from an unhealthy dependence on the automobile industry with its roller-coaster tradition of boom or bust. Great energy was expended to provide distribution centers based on economy-of-scale logic. One of the earliest of these was FoodTerm, opened in Detroit during 1975 for the purpose of handling bulk shipment and transfer of edible liquids such as syrups, fructose, starches, and vegetable oils for beverage companies, bakeries, food processors, and ice cream manufacturers. PolyTerm, a warehouse-transfer facility for bulk plastic pellets, granules, and powders, opened at Warren, Michigan, in 1978. Additional facilities included a one-million-square-foot newsprint warehouse at Ada, Michigan; a distribution center for newsprint and wood pulp at Springfield, Ohio; a coil steel warehouse at Trenton, Michigan; a lumber and plywood distribution center at Taylor, Michigan; and a reload facility for scrap paper and wood pulp at Kalamazoo, Michigan. GTW also provided distribution or "unload/reload" opportunities at Chicago and Grand Rapids. Much of this business moved under contract; indeed, by the end of 1984, 40 percent of all GTW tonnage was billed that way.[25]

There was one area of market development—intermodal—that was at once exhilarating and depressing. Volume increased consistently, and in 1981 revenues in this category

John Burdakin was happy to declare success of expedited service in the vital Chicago–Detroit corridor. New labor agreements helped reduce transit time by up to 50 percent.

were 40 percent above 1980. The question at GTW, and within the industry generally, was twofold: Was this business coming out of boxcars or from highway competitors, and was it compensatory? There was no question at GTW that its traditional boxcar business, especially that related to the cereal and auto industries, was deteriorating—not because of "rail pricing," said Robert Walker, but "as a result of structural and philosophical changes in distribution concepts." Shippers placed emphasis on price, service, and flexibility. Railroads might meet demands of price, but were notoriously inflexible and thus only marginally attuned to service demands. Burdakin insisted that, in partial response to growing modal competition, the realities of deregulation, and pressures from giant rail carriers, GTW "must significantly reduce" its "labor costs to remain competitive" and "look at new business arrangements not restricted to the movement of merchandise freight in boxcars." Cutting costs would be painful and might invite labor unrest; soliciting intermodal business was possible, but would it be remunerative? GTW's route structure—short legs from Port Huron and Detroit to Chicago, and Port Huron and Detroit to Cincinnati—required high costs in train operations and yarding at RailPort (Chicago) and MoTerm (Detroit) without offsetting income from long hauls. Red ink from intermodal operations, a trickle in 1983, was a torrent in 1985. Many managers argued for total discontinuance.[26]

John Burdakin felt himself in a tight spot especially when intermodal issues involved General Motors. GTC managers could not ignore the needs of their largest customer, nor could they ignore the needs of GTC's parent. CN's views regarding intermodal business were undergoing change that certainly would have impact on GTW. In 1985, CN announced massive spending in support of *Laser* service, dedicated new intermodal trains for the 845-mile run between Montreal and Chicago. *Lasers* would feature new motive power and specially designed equipment allowing for heavy loads and would be low enough to allow passage through the Sarnia–Port Huron tunnel. The new trains would operate six days per week on twenty-three-hour schedules, would be handled in the United States by GTW crews, and would yard at Rail-Port in Chicago. Would *Laser* make money for GTW or even cover costs? That remained to be seen. Not at issue, however, was demand, which started strong and got stronger.[27]

Intermodal business was at once exhilarating and depressing. Was it compensatory?

In all seasons, however, the apple of GTW's eye, clearly king of the traffic mix, was automobile business. There was great pleasure at GTW in 1980 when GM announced a huge assembly plant to be built near Pontiac, in 1983 when Chrysler signed an agreement to ship vehicles from a new loading facility in Highland Park, Michigan, and in 1985 when production began at GM's Detroit-Hamtramck assembly plant. There was no pleasure, however, when GM announced reconstruction of its Lansing plant in a way that threatened loss of traffic there to a competitor. That ominous news thoroughly galvanized Gerald Maas, who responded nimbly and worked with GM to design a sophisticated multilevel "direct from the production line" loading facility that served well the needs of the giant automaker and saved the lucrative business for GTW. It was no small accomplishment, Burdakin beamed. The effort received positive comment and earned for GTW the *Modern Railroads* 1985 Golden Freight Car Award in the shipper commitment category.[28]

Maas and Burdakin constantly found themselves in the position of spending appreciable amounts of money to maintain service standards, in some cases, and to improve efficiency, in other cases. New ties and adequate surfacing of track were constants. Burdakin had promoted GTW as the "Good Track Road"; to make good on that assertion required much effort. GTW replaced nearly six million ties and installed 58.2 miles of continuous-welded rail (CWR) in 1980–1982. Track improvements turned downward in 1983–1984, but in 1985 alone GTW installed 52.3 miles of CWR. Monies also were expended to improve and expand communication by replacing trackside pole lines and wire with a microwave system providing high-frequency radio for direct dial long-distance and train-dispatching telephone needs as well as teleprinter and facsimile circuits.[29]

Efficiencies also were gained by upgrading GTW's computer system. An IBM 3033S was acquired in 1981 to replace an IBM 370/148. The new package added capacity necessary, in part, to absorb responsibilities formerly handled by DT&I's computers, shut down subsequent to merger. Capacity was further increased in 1985.[30]

The DT&I shop at Jackson provided a backdrop to the broad issue of labor productivity. After acquisition by GTW, that repair facility was redundant but subject to a 1964 agreement providing severance pay if closed before the passage of twenty years; premature closing would cost $2 million or more. As a consequence, GTW

Gerald Maas took the lead in working out a plan to retain important business from General Motors at Lansing. The effort earned for GTW *Modern Railroads'* 1985 Golden Freight Car Award.

was forced to keep the place open until early 1984, whether there was a need or not. It reflected a broader pattern of labor agreements that had evolved during times when the railroad industry held a virtual modal monopoly or when the industry was fully regulated and thus felt competitive impulses only as they reflected the culture of a particular company—and then almost solely between one railroad and another. Labor and management alike found the 1980s a brave new world, but one that was profoundly frightening at the same time. Was it possible to do business as usual? Business as usual was not good enough—certainly not at GTW. In 1979, a full 61 percent of GTW's expenses came from wages, salaries, and benefits (50 percent was the industry average). That very unattractive figure reflected a sad reality—GTW was out of step. Another statistic was even more depressing. GTW's operating ratio for the six-year period 1980–1986 was a wretched 101 percent.[31]

John Burdakin long had been concerned with the adversarial nature of labor-management relations within the industry and had attempted to "humanize" that relationship, by "adopting a management strategy that stresses long range planning and not spotlighting the current bottom line." This had to be founded on cooperation and communication. "I think it is a good idea to provide people with a complete story" otherwise they are "at the mercy of the rumor mill." And, "generally speaking," said Burdakin at a management meeting on February 3, 1984, "I think we have to get labor more involved and moving in step with us. Railroad people have a special feeling for their industry that may be unmatched in other industries. Railroading indeed 'gets in the blood.' But this reservoir of interest too often gets overlooked in the adversarial relationship that is so prevalent between management and labor. We need to find ways to foster and build on this interest better than we have. One of the best ways to get started is to tell folks what's happening, to bring them into our confidence. They need to hear clearly that our world has changed and that we are going to get leaner and do things more productively than in the past." This, he stressed, would require that employees be "treated as human beings and giving them the consideration and respect that they deserve." Out of it would come, he believed, "employee loyalty and improved productivity." It would be a tough slog.[32]

Change was necessary and change came; its impact, good or bad, depended on one's point of view. Improvements in communication and computer technology reduced the need for telegraph operators and station agents; blending of GTW and DT&I operations meant fewer staff jobs; the closing of Chicago's Elsdon Yard and moving terminal operations to the Belt Railway of Chicago's Clearing Yard claimed many engine, clerk, and switchman jobs; elimination of classification switching at Toledo's Lang Yard and the shutting down of the shops at Jackson cost jobs in several crafts; and reduced crew size and the removal of cabooses on some trains further trimmed GTW employee numbers. All of this fell under the rubric of "cost control." GTC promised "further mechanization of clerical and operations control functions to improve efficiency and . . . [allow] . . . reduced employment." Quite so. And quite necessary. But terribly costly. The whole process was expensive for the company (in machines, technology, and training; in separations payments or relocation costs for personnel) and for employees (in loss of income and benefits). It also exacted a toll in a psychological sense, for change was traumatic for all hands. To his credit, John Burdakin understood the issue. In the main, leaders of unions represented at GTW came to respect him for his vision and convictions. Changes in work rules and other areas became the legacy of this respect. Managers and contract employees alike came to believe as Burdakin did that "the business environment . . . will be progressively less forgiving to industry segments and companies which do not continue to improve productivity."[33]

The need to recognize and meaningfully address new realities, so apparent at Grand Trunk Western, was no less acute at Central Vermont. CV's problems, to an extent, reflected the trials of New England, a region where traffic-producing business was increasingly scarce. The railroad industry suffered accordingly. In the summer of 1982, a thoroughly alarmed John Burdakin had sought opinions regarding CV. After studying the matter, Burdakin and Paul Tatro concluded that CV "under the present corporate structure and political climate" would have "a negative value from both an earnings and cash flow standpoint." A harsh judgment from two dry-eyed analysts. CV went on the market late in 1982. Consequently it was written down to $5 million, "a reasonable sales price," and recorded a $28.9 million loss. The salvage value of CV, Burdakin admitted, exceeded $5 million, but, he concluded, abandonment was not "a viable option available to GTC or CN."[34]

Only three bids were received—one from CV employees, one from a smaller American railroad, and one from unidentified investors. None of the bids was appealing from a monetary point of view, and all prospects demanded traffic guarantees from CN. Staffers in Montreal brooded and eventually concluded that CN's "strategic interest . . . might best be served by keeping CV." As GTC's 1983 annual report dryly noted, CV remained a corporate member.[35]

Blithe comments notwithstanding, CV's future looked bleak. Heads-up management, innovative marketing, and unemotional bargaining to lower costs were essential. General Manager Phillip Larson believed that trailer-on-flat-car (TOFC or piggyback) might hold or regain accounts and so, to that end, CV had instituted dedicated overnight *Rocket* service between Montreal and Palmer, west of Boston, in 1978. A small terminal was provided at Palmer, and the trains attracted positive comment as well as volume. New manufacturing

Central Vermont, despite innovative managers, remained GTC's problem child. (John Gruber photograph.)

plants capable of producing significant carload business were hard to come by, but Phelps Dodge located a large copper wire plant at Yantic, Connecticut. Larson was more successful in attracting several break-bulk distribution centers. Indeed, by the mid-1980s, most of CV's business derived from Canada and moved to distribution centers.[36]

In other areas Larson had mixed results. CV's *Rocket* intermodal service eventually was modified to start from St. Albans, Vermont, instead of Montreal, and extended to New Haven (over Boston & Maine); trailers were trucked to and from St. Albans and New Haven (as well as Palmer). *Rocket* trains were operated with smaller crews and without cabooses, but these reductions in operating costs were inadequate. Competition from truckers, especially from "gypsies," was too much; CV could not raise rates and retain business. *Rocket* service ended in 1984, although intermodal service returned briefly with an outside firm supplying all equipment with CV crews operating the trains. Larson enjoyed much greater success, however, moving woodchips under contract in specially designed hopper cars from Swanton, above St. Albans, to Burlington Electric's generating plant located just east of Burlington, Vermont, thirty-six miles. The deal proved a good one for shipper and carrier alike. Chips were a low-cost, readily available fuel for Burlington Electric, and the efficient use of labor and equipment provided profit for CV. The woodchip train earned *Modern Railroads'* 1985 Golden Freight Car Award in the shipper commitment category.[37]

Phillip Larson also sought ways to make CV a more productive plant. In 1983, agreements were signed with operating crafts that permitted, under conditions of seniority and availability of personnel, train operations with three-person crews—down by one brakeman—and the right to remove cabooses from one-quarter of train movements. It was inadequate. Larson concluded, with Burdakin's firm urging, that CV could not be a party to national labor processes and agreements and in 1984 notified all unions representing CV employees of this decision. Larson would negotiate locally thereafter. At the same time he introduced the "quality circle" concept and practice at St. Albans and New London. All of this represented disruption, change from the usual ways of doing business, and was resisted to some degree by lower-management and contract workers alike. Despite misgivings on many levels, however, all parties pulled in harness when it came to the critical matter of safety in the workplace. CV won prestigious Harriman awards in every year from 1976 through 1981.[38]

As Larson and Burdakin looked back on the first half of the 1980s and ahead to the remaining years of the decade, they had mixed feelings. Both men took pride in CV's physical condition—"the best main line track in northern New England." More important, gross ton-miles and revenue ton-miles increased nicely. But costs outran receipts in some seasons. The operating ratio, 92 in 1980, dropped to 85.5 in 1981 and then raced to a depressing 111.2 in 1984. They were compelled to trim employee numbers; 412 persons were on the payroll in 1980, but only 308 were employed in 1984. The road had total income of $7.6 million for the years 1980–1985, inclusive, but only $5.7 million in operating income. Again it came down to Canadian National—which had to weigh the merits of putting more traffic on Central Vermont against other strategic options.[39]

Canadian National managers and John Burdakin had no similar constraints when it came to Duluth, Winnipeg & Pacific. With ample reason. DW&P produced an average of 2.42 million gross ton-miles annually for the first half of the 1980s; trains averaged a very respectable 6,147 tons. Lumber dominated among traffic commodities, with 35.8 percent of the total, followed by potash (24.9 percent), and paper and wood pulp (16.5 percent). With the vast majority of its business moving from western Canada into the United States, DW&P had little reason for an in-house marketing staff such as that found on CV. Canadian National, instead, handled those duties. The favored connection in 1980 was Chicago & North Western, but during the lengthy Milwaukee acquisition case, DW&P predictably moved more business to CMStP&P; in 1985, with consummation of the new VCA, Burlington Northern got the nod.[40]

DW&P's principal yard expenses were at the Head of the Lakes, where its vest-pocket West Duluth facility hugged a rugged escarpment overlooking the St. Louis River Valley and Lake Superior. Yard tracks were not level and tilted dangerously toward the lake, and to get from West Duluth to connections required impressive but extremely expensive trestlework plus trackage rights. Traditionally, road crews handled trains only into and out of West Duluth, with yard crews required to move cuts to and from connections. DW&P's terminal operation was, in sum, operationally difficult and expensive; it also caused irksome delay to lading and added car hire cost.

Duluth, Winnipeg & Pacific remained, as always, a very profitable "hook & haul" railroad.

Throughout the 1970s, those responsible for DW&P's welfare brooded about problems at Duluth. Nevertheless, they were loath to move quickly since they knew that Minnesota transportation authorities were contemplating an extension of the Interstate Highway System that likely was to have an impact on all rail operations downtown and in the industrialized area along the lake. Meanwhile, Gene Shepard and other DW&P managers looked for property across the way in Wisconsin for a new yard and talked with other railroaders about opportunities to rationalize plant and means by which to expedite traffic moving among the several carriers. Finally, in 1979, a verbal agreement was made with highway authorities, but progress was slow; negotiations were required with three cities, two states, and six railroads. Burdakin was kept apprised throughout, but he had full and appropriate faith in his onsite people and he gave them their head. The wait was tedious, but the anguish was worth it. In 1981, DW&P management was given the green signal to make all arrangements necessary to move from West Duluth to Pokegama, near Superior, Wisconsin, and to join in trackage/yardage/interchange agreements with cooperating roads. John Burdakin and DW&P officers, in public and in private, referred to the move as "forced" by the "I-35 highway relocation project," but in reality they were overjoyed by the new arrangement—especially since the federal government through the state of Minnesota would reimburse most of the cost ($15,490,000 of $18,511,000). Work began in 1983 on the eighteen-track yard and on connections with

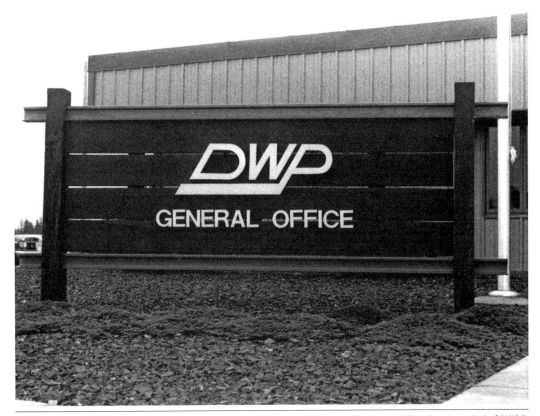

The new facility at Pokegema opened on December 1, 1984. It was spartan yet attractive and functional—typical of DW&P. (Don L. Hofsommer photograph.)

Duluth, Missabe & Iron Range Railway (DM&IR) to reach tracks and yards of Burlington Northern (which CMStP&P also used), Soo Line in Superior, and Chicago & North Western at Itasca, as well as with DM&IR to Nopeming Junction, milepost 10.5, and a junction there with DW&P's route to Virginia and Ranier. Forces from the accounting department in downtown Duluth and all departments from West Duluth moved to the handsome new Pokegema facility on December 1, 1984; revenue trains began use of Pokegema six days later. The entire property was spartan yet attractive and functional—typical of DW&P.[41]

The company's motto, "Delivered With Pride," proved to be more than boastful rhetoric. DW&P's small workforce (389 persons in 1980, 291 in 1984) produced extremely efficient transportation; the operating ratio for the first half of the 1980s averaged a very respectable 80.3. Sophisticated computers and communications systems included a system-wide microwave network that aided DW&P personnel and shippers alike. More hotbox/dragging detectors, persistent tie renewal programs, additional welded rail, and a fleet of General Motors SD-40 locomotives carefully maintained by DW&P mechanical forces spelled reliability that was noticed by customers and connecting carriers alike. Productivity was enhanced by the introduction of unit trains of potash in 1980, and in 1985 by granting trackage rights to Burlington Northern over 153 miles to Ranier (giving DW&P added revenue and allowing BN to abandon its own line to International Falls). Employee morale was heightened by knowledge that the company had a policy of constantly spending money to improve the property, and this was well and properly reflected in DW&P's safety record: Harriman awards in 1978, 1980, 1983, and 1984.[42]

Had Robert A. Bandeen's Grand Trunk Corporation experiment run out of steam? The picture was unclear.

DW&P's excellent record was best reflected by its income statements. The road had total net income of $21 million for the five-year period 1980–1984. DW&P was, in fact, the heart of the GTC concept. Losses at GTW, and more recently at CV, served to shelter DW&P's income; DW&P had also been used to provide cross-guarantees for debts incurred by GTW. All of this was necessary since CN had determined that GTW was an essential component but one that could no longer receive cash infusions from the parent. DW&P, through GTC, in effect replaced CN as GTW's financial backbone. It was a practical arrangement by which CN's investment and marketing requirements in the American properties could be protected. And in the 1970s, GTC had been profitable—by $53,754,000. The deep recession of the early 1980s proved disastrous, however; GTC lost $53.8 million (of which $27.5 million was for the write-down of CV).[43]

Had Bandeen's experiment run out of steam? The picture was unclear. GTC celebrated its fourteenth birthday in 1984 and had been profitable in all but four of those years. But the very author of GTC, Robert A. Bandeen, was no longer around to champion the cause. What would this mean ultimately for GTC? Bandeen had been predictably popular with managers and directors of the GTC roads. He was "one of the greatest things ever to come down the pike," said an unabashed William K. Smith, vice president of General Mills and a GTW director. CN's Ron Lawless credited Bandeen with "letting managers do their own thing," and stressed that he had been "impressive in the strategic development of the company." After Bandeen's departure, GTC managers were apprehensive. After all, Bandeen had stood in the breach between GTC's independent management and the forces of tradition so enwrapped at Montreal. "Bandeen was the insulation," as GTW's Earl C. Opperthauser observed.[44]

Chapter 9

A Great Ride

CANADIAN NATIONAL HAD A POLICY OF MANDATORY RETIREMENT AT AGE SIXTY-FIVE, and by the end of 1985 John Burdakin was racing toward that target. He took predictable pride that year when Grand Trunk Western and Central Vermont both took home *Modern Railroads'* prestigious Golden Freight Car awards for their respective marketing innovations. He took even greater pride in nine Harriman Safety Awards that Grand Trunk Corporation roads had collected since 1980. After all, the first requirement found in every operating rule book read: "Safety is of the first importance in the discharge of duty." Lax company support for safe practice and/or lax attention to safe practice inevitably led to accidents and often reflected poor morale among the workforce. Burdakin clearly understood the tight connection between a tidy workplace, employee morale, and safe practice. "Paint up, fix up, clean up," coupled with hearty emphasis on being a "good-track railroad," was his mantra. First monies went to the plant. All hands took note. If managers took pride in property, so did contract employees. Morale reflected this. So did safe practice.[1]

Burdakin's particular interest in safety no doubt was stoked by his exposure to and his vivid recollection of the awful accident at Coshocton, Ohio, during his time at Pennsylvania Railroad. That devotion only deepened at Grand Trunk Western after locomotive fireman Hank Kohl was run over by wayward boxcars and lost an arm and two legs. Burdakin went to the hospital with claim agent Art Fettig to visit the most unfortunate Kohl. Burdakin was much taken with Kohl's grit in facing his new reality but much chagrined that such a nasty incident should happen on his watch. Out of this would come an ever greater advocacy for safe practice, the need to keep the issue before all employees (especially in the operating crafts), and appointment of Fettig as employee communication officer.[2]

As shadows lengthened for John Burdakin at Grand Trunk Corporation, he found time to reflect on his management approach. He was, he said, "proud of his ability to select individuals that have a feeling of responsibility, to take responsibility for their position and perform to the best of their abilities"—in other words:

> to select generally the right person for the job. Eventually some may have disappointed me, but basically when I promoted somebody, I was confident that I had an individual who could perform well, and history has indicated that I was reasonably successful at that. I also feel that my approach

to both people above me and below me was one of a factual, straightforward style. If they asked my opinion, they got my best opinion. If I agreed with what they were saying, I would say so. If I disagreed, I would say so, and I would have my own reasons for it.

Again, I feel I had a good understanding of a subordinate's position. They knew they had an individual who would back them up. If I approved their proposal, then it would be my responsibility.

If it went bad, I was responsible. They knew they wouldn't get their neck chopped off. I very definitely tried not to criticize anybody who was going forward and doing something. I would be more critical of somebody standing still and not moving.

Maybe I was not the most original manager in the world, but at least a manager who would support subordinates and one who was looking for progress, one who was looking for change . . . progress . . . moving forward . . . improvement of the operation.[3]

Asked to give his opinion as to prime managerial attributes, Burdakin responded in machine-gun fashion, a wry, crackly smile on his face.

1. Competence ("Know what you are supposed to do")
2. Truthfulness ("No happy horseshit")
3. Forthrightness ("Don't try to snowball")
4. People skills ("Everybody has a place someplace. Get along with people.")
5. Teaching skills ("No pomposity. Treat people like people.")[4]

John Burdakin always emphasized safe practice and took understandable pride when GTC roads won Harriman awards.

How effective was Burdakin himself as a teacher? What did others learn from him? For Marc Higginbotham it was the need to be "positive, forward thinking, strength of character, and *absolute* integrity as an individual and leader of an organization." Gene Shepard pointed to "setting high standards (professional and personal) and letting good managers manage and helping those who need it." James A. Brewer felt it was "the strong work ethic"; Gloria Combe underscored "respect and fairness for others"; Virginia Czarnik said "concern for all employees"; and Veronica Cabble emphasized "integrity—do your very best—never say 'can't.'" For Howard D. Nicholas it was "lead by example"; for Jim Krikau it was "never to compromise one's values—apply your belief systems consistently"; for Howard M. Tischler it was "to be an honest and empowering manager—to view individuals on their own merits." Phillip C. Larson learned much about "railroad engineering, budgets, and dealing with people," while Charles Hrdlicka focused on "dedication in purpose and strength in leadership." Ronald L. Batory had a long list: "Lead by example. Never walk by a mistake. Facts over opinion. Money spent wisely is more important than the amount of money spent. Never fear failure (it breeds a unique experience of learning). Never resist the opportunity to be a change agent." William J. McKnight likewise put forward a lengthy list. "Keep up to date with your work, don't let paperwork languish, try to keep a neat desk, return phone calls, don't lose your temper, treat people as you'd like to be treated, keep your promises, tend to relationships." Several persons were utterly stark in relating what they had learned from him and the tight assessment of his impact on them. "He was the best boss I ever had," said both Gene Shepard and Phillip Larson. "John Burdakin is a man's man and a railroader's railroader" was the bold and vivid view of Ronald Batory. "I view John Burdakin as a great example of an ethical and honorable individual and manager," argued Howard Tischler, "who should be held up as a model in the North American business world." Is it too much to say, on the basis of this rather small sample, that John Burdakin was an influential and effective teacher for those who worked with him? Absolutely not.[5]

John Burdakin did not look forward to his departure from leadership of the Grand Trunk Corporation roads. It was hard to let go. His father so many years ago had admonished him to "do something you want to do and do the best you can." Railroading had been his career, he had wanted that career, and he had done the best he could. In particular he was proud of his impact on the fortunes of Grand Trunk Western—bringing it "from a weak, basically insolvent railroad into a recognized, strongly managed U.S. Class One property." Others took note. Burdakin was inducted into the Michigan Transportation Hall of Fame—the first railroader so honored. Still others, within and without the company, rendered their own dry-eyed assessment of Burdakin's stewardship. They argued in chorus: "Grand Trunk Corporation was brilliantly conceived by Robert Bandeen, and John Burdakin made it work."[6]

Effective January 1, 1986, Gerald Maas, executive vice president of Grand Trunk Western since 1984, became president of the Grand Trunk Corporation properties. Burdakin was named vice chairman of GTC. "This management shift assures continuity and strength for Grand Trunk," said Canadian National's J. Maurice LeClair, "at a time when the American railroad industry is in the midst of rapid change." In a dramatic example of understatement, the GTC annual report for 1986 simply said of Burdakin that "his record has enhanced the strengths and reputation of Grand Trunk Corporation." Indeed. Burdakin's last day on the payroll was August 11, 1987. Retirement festivities at the Detroit Athletic Club followed a month later.[7]

While his eye never got far from the railroad, retirement did have allure. Now, finally, he could share extended time with his wonderful wife Jean and pay closer attention to their boys

Perhaps Burdakin's greatest accomplishment was taking Grand Trunk Western "from a weak, basically insolvent railroad into a recognized, strongly managed U.S. Class One property."

and their families. And there was time for golf and woodworking and for volunteer work with Jean in various capacities, including teaching English as a second language, "pushing wheelchairs" at local hospitals, and taking on chores at church. Sad to say, John lost his "dear companion for over 63 years" when Jean died in 2012.[8]

Three times annually, Grand Trunk retirees meet for lunch at the Sign of the Beef Carver in Royal Oak, Michigan—this for the purpose of seeing one another, of camaraderie, of recalling days now gone by, and of simply having a good time. On September 5, 2013, nearly seventy of them showed up to greet "Mr. Burdakin," who at the age of ninety-one was "overwhelmed by the large number of people who came out to see an old railroader." He recalled that when he arrived at Grand Trunk he "found good, solid, hardworking people" who, he underscored, "came to my rescue many times." Burdakin said he had "great respect for any of whom he had mentored in any way," and, his voice trailing off, feared he had not adequately praised persons when that praise was due. "I hope that some of my principles and practices have been spread among others"—"especially how to treat people." Finally, he said, "It was a great ride for me on the Grand Trunk because of the close relationship with people like you."[9]

It was vintage John Howard Burdakin. His founding and everlasting principles on full display.

John Howard Burdakin.

Notes

CHAPTER 1. A CONTRIBUTIVE AND CONSTRUCTIVE LIFE

1. John H. Burdakin, farewell remarks, September 11, 1987, from author's collection.

CHAPTER 2. FIRM FOUNDATIONS

1. John H. Burdakin, interview, July 23, 1994, John W. Barriger III National Railroad Library, St. Louis, MO. Hereinafter cited as Interview, July 23, 1994.
2. Ibid.
3. Ibid.
4. Ibid.; John H. Burdakin, interview by the author, June 5, 2013.
5. Burdakin, interview, June 5, 2013.
6. Burdakin, interview, July 23, 1994.
7. Ibid.
8. Ibid.
9. Ibid.
10. Ibid.; Burdakin, interview, June 10, 2013.
11. Burdakin, interview, July 23, 1994.
12. Ibid.
13. Ibid.
14. Ibid.
15. Burdakin, interview, June 5, 2013.
16. Burdakin, interviews, July 23, 1994, June 5, 10, 2013; Jean Burdakin, "My Life: Stories for My Children," unpublished manuscript, 2001.
17. Burdakin, interviews, July 23, 1994, June 5, 10, 2013.

CHAPTER 3. THE STANDARD RAILROAD OF THE WORLD

1. John H. Burdakin, interview, July 23, 1994.
2. Ibid.
3. John H. Burdakin, "My Saddest Day Railroading," unpublished manuscript, n.d.

4. Burdakin, interview, July 23, 1994.

5. Ibid.; Burdakin, interview, June 6, 2013.

6. Burdakin, interview, July 23, 1994.

7. Burdakin, interview, June 5, 2013.

8. Ibid.

9. Burdakin, interview, November 21, 2013.

10. Burdakin, interview, July 23, 1994.

11. Burdakin, interviews, June 13, November 25, 2013.

12. Burdakin, interview, July 23, 1994.

13. Ibid.

14. Burdakin, interview, June 6, 2013.

15. Gloria Combe, interview, July 15, 2013; Larry Baggerly, interview, July 15, 2013.

16. Burdakin, interview, June 6, 2013.

CHAPTER 4. OUT OF CANADA

1. Burdakin, interviews, June 5, 6, 2013.

2. Ibid.

3. On Canadian National, see Henry Eldon Hewetson, *The Financial History of the Canadian National Railway* (Chicago: University of Chicago Press, 1946); George R. Stevens, *Canadian National Railways*, 2 vols. (Toronto: Clarke, Irwin, 1960); Stevens, *History of the Canadian National Railways* (New York: Macmillan, 1973); John H. Burdakin, interviews May 24, November 4, 1989; Robert A. Bandeen, interview, November 3, 1989; Grand Trunk Western, Minute Book No. 4, 17, 29, 45, 59, 69, 79.

4. GTW, Minute Book No. 4, 85.

5. Merrill Shepard, telex to R. A. Bandeen, November 1969; John Guest telex to CNR, December 3, 1969.

6. GTW, Minutes of Executive Committee, November 30, 1970; R. A. Bandeen, memorandum to N. J. MacMillan, November 11, 1970.

7. GTW, Executive Minute No. 531; G. M. Cooper to J. W. G. Macdougall, August 4, 1971.

8. Stevens, *History*, 455; John H. Burdakin, interview, February 21, 1989.

9. John H. Burdakin, interviews, December 6, 1988, November 4, 1989.

10. Burdakin, interview, June 6, 2013.

11. Burdakin, interview, November 25, 2013.

12. Burdakin, interview, November 4, 1989; GTC, Annual Report, 1973, 2–3; Jonathan Hughes, *American Economic History*, 3rd ed. (Glenview: Scott Foresman, 1990), 589–592; John F. Willis and Martin L. Primack, *An Economic History of the United States*, 2nd ed. (Englewood Cliffs, NJ: Prentice Hall, 1989), 417–419.

13. *GT Reporter*, March–April 1973, 1; Burdakin, interview, November 4, 1989.

14. CN, Overview—Grand Trunk Western (Montreal), July 1969, 64–65; GTW, Minute Book No. 4, 122; *GT Reporter*, May 1971, 1; GTW, Minute Book No. 5, 1971 Financial Results, 6; GTC, Annual Report, 1972, 29.

15. CN, Synoptical History, 275–278; GTW, Minute Book No. 6, Executive Minute No. 539; GTW, Minute Book No. 5, 195–196; GTW, Minute Book No. 5, 1972 Financial Results, 8.

16. Tabular data from GTC annual reports, 1972–1975.

17. Bandeen, interview, November 3, 1989; *GT Reporter*, March–April 1974, 1; CN, Annual Report, 1974, 15.

18. *Chicago Tribune*, November 7, 1971; *GT Reporter*, September–October 1974, 1; Bandeen, interview, November 3, 1989.

19. GTC, Annual Report, 1972, 2; Robert A. Bandeen, interview, March 7, 1990; Earl C. Opperthauser, interview, November 6, 1989.

20. Stanley H. Mailer, "In Minnesota CN Is Spelled DW&P," *Trains* 34 (March 1974), 20–28; GTC, Annual Reports, 1972, 2; 1973, 17, 21; DW&P, Corporate Records Book No. 3, Executive Minute No. 15; GTC, Annual Report, 1974, 10.

21. GTC, Annual Report, 1972, 9–15; GTC, Annual Report, 1973, 8–15; GTC, Annual Report, 1974, 13–16; GTC, Annual Report, 1975, 13–16.

22. GTW, Minute Book No. 5, 1971 Financial Results, 8; GTC, Annual Report, 1972, 3; GTW, Executive Committee Book No. 7, Executive Minute No. 565; GTC, Annual Reports, 1973, 3, 1974, 25.

23. *GT Reporter*, March–April 1974, 1.

CHAPTER 5. A PATIENT APPROACH

1. CN, Annual Report, 1975, 7.

2. Ibid.

3. Ronald L. Lawless, interview, August 7, 1989; Yvon H. Masse, interview, May 24, 1989; Bandeen, interview, November 3, 1989.

4. CN, Annual Report, 1970, 46; tabular data from CN annual reports.

5. John H. Burdakin to the author, October 11, 2013.

6. CN, Synoptical History, 291; GTW, Minute Book No. 4, 122; *GT Reporter*, November–December 1974, 5; *GT Reporter*, August–September 1977, 3.

7. On the century-old rail-marine operation on the Great Lakes, see George W. Hilton, *The Great Lakes Car Ferries* (Berkeley: Howell-North, 1962); *Railway Age* 150 (March 27, 1961), 30–31; CN, Synoptical History, 331–335, 432–433.

8. CN, Overview—Grand Trunk Western, 68–69.

9. Ibid., 70–74.

10. J. A. Elliott, "A Proposal Concerning the Grand Trunk Western Car Ferry Service," 1972, 1–52; GTW, Minute Book No. 5, 1971 Financial Results, 7; George W. Hilton, "Great Lakes Ferries: An Endangered Species," *Trains* 35 (January 1975), 42–51; *GT Reporter*, April 1978, 1; ICC, Certificate and Decision, Docket No. AB-31 (Sub. No. 5), October 31, 1978; Grand Trunk Milwaukee Car Ferry Company, Minute Book, 221.

11. Opperthauser, interview, November 6, 1989; GTC, Annual Report, 1976, 4–5; G. B. Aydelott, interview, February 9, 1990.

12. GTW, Minute Book No. 7, 301, 323; GTC, Annual Report, 1979, 8; *GT Reporter*, November–December 1975, 3.

13. GTW, Minute Book No. 6, 229, 237; *GT Reporter*, November–December 1976, 2; GTC, Annual Report, 1976, 22.

14. GTW, Minute Book No. 5, 178; *GT Reporter*, November–December 1973, 5.

15. CN, Synoptical History, 298–299; GTW, Minute Book No. 5, 1971 Financial Results, 8; GTW, Minute Book No. 7, 284.

16. Luther S. Miller, "CN: Productivity Is the Road to Profits, and CN Rail Is Showing the Way," *Railway Age* 179 (December 25, 1978), 22–30.

17. *GT Reporter*, May 1977, 1.

18. GTC, Annual Report 1977, 1, 13.

19. GTC, Annual Reports, 1977, 10–12; 1978, 12; 1980, 14.

20. GTC, Annual Report, 1976, 1; DW&P, Executive Committee Book, Executive Minute No. 27.

21. GTC, Annual Reports, 1976, 9; 1978, 10.

22. Thomas J. Lamphier, interview, March 29, 1989; James R. Sullivan, interview, February 9, 1990; GTC, Annual Report, 1972, 26; *GT Reporter*, August–September 1977, 1; GTC, Annual Report, 1977, 6; *GT Reporter*, May–June 1974, 1; August 1978, 1.

23. *GT Reporter*, September–October 1973, 6, September–October 1975, 2; GTC, Annual Report, 1976, 5; *GT Reporter*, October–November 1978, 2–3; GTW, Minute Book No. 7, 291; GTC, Annual Reports, 1978, 7, 1979, 8; GTC, Annual Report, 1972, 32; *GT Reporter*, May–June 1974, 1; *Railway Age* 179 (December 25, 1978), 50–51; GTC, Annual Report, 1976, 5.

24. John H. Burdakin, "Grand Trunk Western Railroad Corporate Objectives," February 1975; Lawless, interview, August 7, 1989.

25. Tabular data from GTC annual reports, 1972–1979.

26. Gus Welty, "Grand Trunk Western: Battling toward Profitability," *Railway Age* 176 (September 8, 1975), 30–32, 104; Tom Shedd, "Freedom Pays," *Modern Railroads*, July 1976, 20–23; *Railway Age* 179 (December 25, 1978), 27; Bill Palmer, "CN's American Brother," *CN Movin,'* March–April 1977, 4–7.

27. GTC, Annual Report, 1979, 8.

CHAPTER 6. TAKING STOCK

1. H. Roger Grant, *Erie Lackawanna: Death of an American Railroad, 1938–1992* (Stanford: Stanford University Press, 1994), 172–174, 195–217; Albro Martin, *Railroads Triumphant: The Growth, Rejection, and Rebirth of a Vital American Force* (New York: Oxford University Press, 1992), 388; Richard Saunders, *Main Lines: Rebirth of the North American Railroads, 1970–2002* (DeKalb: Northern Illinois University Press, 2003), 112–115; John H. Burdakin, presentation to Canadian National board of directors, Montreal, October 25, 1976.

2. Burdakin, interview, July 23, 1994.

3. Ibid.

4. Ibid.; John H. Burdakin to Joseph V. McDonald, n.d.; John H. Burdakin, remarks at GTC board dinner, November 19, 1979; *GT Reporter* 10 (March 1975), 1.

5. Palmer, "CN's American Brother"; John H. Burdakin, presentation to Canadian National board of directors, Montreal, September 21, 1976.

6. *GT Reporter* 10 (May–June 1975), 1; John H. Burdakin, presentation to the Canadian National board of directors, Montreal, September 21, 1976; GTC, Annual Report, 1976, 1.

7. John H. Burdakin, presentation to the Canadian National board of directors, Montreal, September 21, 1976.

8. Burdakin, interview, June 6, 2013; *GT Reporter* 11 (April–May 1976), 6; Gloria Combe, interview, December 4, 2013.

9. Combe, interview, December 4, 2013.

10. *GT Reporter*, May–June 1973, 1–2; GTW, Minute Book No. 5, 159; GTC, Annual Report, 1974, 7.

11. GTC, Annual Reports, 1975, 7, 1976, 5, 1977, 3, 1979, 8; Gus Welty, "Mandatory AEI Tagging," *Railway Age* 192 (March 1991), 34–38.

12. Richard Saunders, *The Railroad Mergers and the Coming of Conrail* (Westport: Greenwood Press, 1978), 301, 308, 315, 319, 324, 325.

13. Basil Cole, interview, March 21, 1989.

14. Robert A. Walker, interview, March 7, 1990; GTW, Minute Book No. 5, 193; GTW, "USRA/Conrail: Give Michigan's Smaller Railroads a Chance to Compete," 1975.

15. *GT Reporter*, April 1975, 1; USRA, *Final System Plan*, 2 vols. (Washington, DC: Government Printing Office, 1975), 1:26–27, 234, 269–299, 359, 365, 2:171–179, 189–199; GTW, Minute Book No. 6, 219, 227; GTC, Annual Report, 1976, 24; GTW, Minute Book No. 7, 310.

16. William D. Middleton, "Henry Ford and His Electric Locomotives," *Trains* 36 (September 1976), 22–26; Scott D. Trostel, *The Detroit, Toledo & Ironton Railroad: Henry Ford's Railroad* (Fletcher: Cam-Tech, 1998).

17. DT&I, Financial Planning Study by Salomon Brothers, 1975, 103.

18. DT&I, Corporate Records 16, April 22, June 30, September 17, October 27, 1976.

19. Ibid.; Robert A. Sharp, interview, May 3, 1989.

20. Robert A. Bandeen to John H. Burdakin, February 28, 1977; John H. Burdakin to Robert A. Bandeen, March 2, 1977; *Wall Street Journal*, May 31, June 13, 1977.

21. GTW, Press Releases, October 24, 1977, January 5, 1978; Basil Cole, interview, June 14, 1994.

22. GTC, Annual Report, 1977, 3; GTW, Minute Book No. 7, 277–278; GTC, Application, Finance Docket 28499, February 16, 1978.

23. Cole, interview, March 21, 1989; Saunders, *Railroad Mergers*, 325; John H. Burdakin, interview, March 5, 1991; *Lansing State Journal*, September 17, 1978.

24. Post Hearing Brief for Pennsylvania Company and Detroit, Toledo & Ironton Railroad, May 21, 1979, 12, 45, 47.

25. N&W/Chessie, Brief of Joint Applicants to Administrative Law Judge Richard H. Beddow Jr., May 21, 1979, 2, 20, 23, 81, 83.

26. Brief of Canadian National Railway Company to Administrative Law Judge Beddow, May 21, 1979; Robert A. Bandeen to John H. Burdakin, February 28, 1977; N&W/Chessie brief, 64; PC/DT&T, Post-Hearing Brief for Pennsylvania Company and Detroit, Toledo & Ironton Railroad Company, May 21, 1979, 46.

27. N&W/Chessie Brief, 70; Verified Statement of John F. Burdakin, June 27, 1978.

28. *Railway Age*, November 27, 1979, 13–14, April 30, 1979, 9, July 27, 1981, 24–27, September 12, 1982, 12–13.

29. Cole, interview, March 21, 1989; Robert vom Eigen, interview, March 21, 1989.

30. DT&I, Corporate Records 27, December 6, 1979, February 28, 1980; and 28, March 10, 1980; GTW, Minute Book No. 7, 327; DT&I, Corporate Records 25, April 1, 1980; 363 ICC 122–131; DT&I, Corporate Records 30, 1–5.

31. GTW, Executive Committee Book No. 8, Executive Minute No. 639; GTW, Minute Book No. 89, 357–358; D&TSL, Minute Book No. 5, 786–805.

CHAPTER 7. JILTED

1. On the history of the Milwaukee Road, see August Derleth, *The Milwaukee Road: Its First Hundred Years* (New York: Creative Age Press, 1948); *Trains* 51 (November 1990), 39–41.

2. Jim Scribbins, "Interview with John H. Burdakin," *Milwaukee Railroader* 18 (September 1988), 4–7.

3. *Railway Age* 192 (January 12, 1981), 8; *First Monday / Third Monday*, December 15, 1980; F. Stewart Mitchell, "Milwaukee II: A Transformation of Assets," *Modern Railroads* 36 (August 1981), 47–48.

4. Trustee's Revised Plan of Reorganization, Finance Docket No. 28640, September 15, 1981, 1–28; *Railway Age* 182 (September 28, 1981), 12.

5. John H. Burdakin to John S. Guest, June 23, 1980; John H. Burdakin to E. R. Adams et al., June 23, 1980 (PF 150).

6. Milwaukee Road Press Release, October 27, 1981; *Wall Street Journal*, October 28, 1981; Scribbins, "Interview with Burdakin," 4.

7. *Wall Street Journal*, October 28, 1981.

8. *Chicago Tribune*, November 1, 1981; *New York Journal of Commerce*, November 3, 1981.

9. GTC, "Acquisition Evaluation Chicago, Milwaukee, St. Paul & Pacific Railroad Company," February 2, 1982; GTC, "GTC and Milwaukee II Objectives Can Be Achieved through Cooperative Action," February 2, 1982 (PF 107).

10. GTC, "Results of GTC/CN Study of Chicago, Milwaukee, St. Paul & Pacific Railroad Company, February 15, 1982 (PF 107).

11. *Trains* 42 (August 1982), 8–10; *New York Times*, May 26, 1982.

12. GTC, Press Release, May 24, 1982; *Railway Age* 183 (June 14, 1982), 26; *Modern Railroads* 37 (June 1982), 10.

13. *Railway Age* 183 (October 5, 1982), 4; *Wall Street Journal*, February 3, 1983; *First Monday / Third Monday*, November 1, 1982.

14. *Railway Age* 180 (December 31, 1979), 23–29; 181 (December 28, 1980), 14; *Modern Railroads* 35 (January 1980), 17.

15. *Des Moines Register*, September 15, 1982; *Kansas City Business Journal*, November 22, 28, 1982; *Modern Railroads* 37 (October 1982), 10.

16. Byron D. Olsen to the author, October 11, 1991; Dennis M. Cavanaugh, interview, September 17, 1991.

17. *Chicago Tribune*, January 26, 1983; *Modern Railroads* 38 (April 1983), 7; 38 (June 1983), 11; *Des Moines Register*, June 9, 1983.

18. E. Maroti to J. Burdakin, June 28, 1983 (PF 950).

19. *Kansas City Business Journal*, July 4, 10, 1983; *Railway Age* 185 (April 1984), 62–63.

20. Soo Line, Second Quarter Report, 1983; *Chicago Tribune*, January 9, 26, 1983.

21. Cole, interview, March 21, 1989; Scribbins, "Interview with Burdakin," 5; *Railway Age* 183 (September 13, 1982), 4; John H. Burdakin to Richard D. Ogilvie, October 11, 1982 (PF 950).

22. Trustee's Amended Plan of Reorganization, March 31, 1983.

23. *Wall Street Journal*, July 29, November 9, 1983.

24. Scribbins, "Interview with Burdakin," 7; Amended Plan of Reorganization, appendix 4, 4, 6, 8; *Chicago Tribune*, July 29, 1983; *Crane's Chicago Business*, August 1, 1983.

25. *Des Moines Register*, September 14, 1983; *Milwaukee Sentinel*, November 1, 1983.

26. *Green Bay News Chronicle*, October 25, 1983; *Minneapolis Star Tribune*, November 1, 1983; *Des*

Moines Register, November 6, 1983; *Chicago Tribune*, November 13, 1983; Amended Plan of Reorganization, appendix 1, 59, 68, 136.

27. Soo Line, Third Quarter Report, 1983; *Chicago Tribune*, December 14, 1983; *Wall Street Journal*, January 20, February 8, 21, 1984; *New York Journal of Commerce*, February 8, 1984.

28. *Chicago Tribune*, March 1, 27, April 16, 1984; *Wall Street Journal*, March 1, April 7, 16, 1984; *Railway Age* 185 (April 1984), 21; *New York Journal of Commerce*, July 12, 1984; Byron Olsen, "Milwaukee Road's Rescue," *Trains* 73 (April 2013), 38–47.

29. ICC, Official Transcript, F.D. 28640, July 26, 1984, 8, 14, 42, 50.

30. Ibid., 1–30; *Minneapolis Star Tribune*, July 27, 1984; *Wall Street Journal*, September 11, 1984.

31. *Minneapolis Tribune*, October 11, 1984; *Wall Street Journal*, October 17, 19, 30, 1984, February 11, 1985; *Business Week*, February 25, 1985, 34; *Railway Age* 186 (March 1985), 27; Soo Line, Special Report to Shareholders, February 21, 1995.

32. Ogilvie was fond of using the term "truly a marriage made in heaven," and is quoted thusly in the *Chicago Tribune*, March 27, 1984; Cole, interview, March 21, 1989; Robert P. vom Eigen, interview, March 22, 1989.

33. Burdakin, interviews, July 23, 1994, June 5, 6, 2013.

34. Ibid.

CHAPTER 8. SOLDIERING ON

1. Discussion among William J. McKnight, Marc H. Higginbotham, Gene Shepard, Annette M. Duffany, and Gloria R. Combe at Livonia, Michigan on September 4, 2013.

2. Ibid.

3. Ibid.

4. John H. Burdakin, address before the American Railway Engineering Association, Chicago, March 22, 1982; John H. Burdakin to the author, July 26, 1994.

5. Communications from those cited to the author.

6. Ibid.

7. McKnight et al., discussion.

8. James F. Willis and Martin L. Primack, *An Economic History of the United States*, 2nd ed. (Englewood Cliffs: Prentice Hall, 1989), 417–437; Hughes, *American Economic History*, 589–597.

9. Robert Roberts, "Deregulation: The Turning Point," *Modern Railroads* 35 (December 1980), 58–62; F. Stewart Mitchell, "Loosening the Grip," *Modern Railroads* 36 (April 1981), 34–35; Frank D. Shaffer, "We Now Have the Tools," *Modern Railroads* 36 (April 1981), 36–39; Frank Malone, "Contract Rates Are Catching On," *Railway Age* 183 (February 22, 1982), 42–44; Gus Welty, "Change!" *Railway Age* 185 (January 1984), 37–44.

10. G. B. Aydelott, interview, September 22, 1982; *New York Journal of Commerce*, June 17, 1982, March 22, 1983; *Wall Street Journal*, February 22, July 3, 1983.

11. *Railroad Facts* (Washington, DC: Association of American Railroads, 1984), 32.

12. Don L. Hofsommer, *The Southern Pacific, 1901–1985* (College Station: Texas A&M University Press, 1986), 302–303; Vance Richardson, "A Marriage of Equals," *CSX Quarterly*, Fall 1990, 9–25; *Railway Age* 183 (September 12, 1982), 11–13; Gus Welty, "The Meaning of Merger," *Railway Age* 185 (July 1984), 73–76; GTW, Minute Book No. 8, 355–356; *Modern Railroads* 37 (June 1982), 10.

13. Welty, "The Meaning of Merger."

14. GTW, Minute Book No. 9, 472; *GT Reporter*, August 1985, 1; John H. Burdakin to Hon. Donald W. Riegel Jr., June 19, 1985 (PF 108).

15. GTC, Annual Report, 1985, 6–7; John H. Burdakin to Hon. John H. Riley, January 10, 1986; John H. Riley to John H. Burdakin, November 19, 1985; *Journal of Commerce*, February 3, 1986; Hon. John H. Dingell to Hon. Elizabeth Hanford Dole, February 7, 1986; John H. Burdakin to Hon. John C. Danforth, June 19, 1985.

16. *Railway Age* 186 (February 1985), 23.

17. *GT Reporter*, August 1985, 1; *New York Times*, June 17, 1985; Conrail, Annual Report, 1986, 1–2; GTC, Annual Report, 1986, 5.

18. Walter H. Cramer to John H. Burdakin, May 23, 1979 (PF 108); Don L. Hofsommer, *The Quanah Route: A History of the Quanah, Acme & Pacific Railway* (College Station: Texas A&M University Press, 1991), 183.

19. GTC, Annual Report, 1985, 10; *GT Reporter*, May 1983, 1; Agreement between Consolidated Rail Corporation and Grand Trunk Western Railroad Company, December 18, 1975; John H. Burdakin to W. H. Cramer and G. L. Maas, November 12, 1982 (PF 108); *Modern Railroads* 38 (August 1983), 9; GTW, "Are Giant Rail Systems Foreclosing Rail Competition? A Grand Trunk Point of View," 1983.

20. Opperthauser, interview, November 6, 1989; ICC, Changes in Routing Provisions—Conrail—July 1981, Docket No. 38676, September 5, 1986; John C. Danielson to Carl V. Lyon, October 17, 1986 (PF 108).

21. Affidavit of Peter C. White, October 5, 1984 (PF 108).

22. GTC, Executive Briefing Summary, August 21, 1984; GTC, Minute Book No. 3, 192–193; *Detroit Free Press*, September 6, 1984; John H. Burdakin to R. E. Lawless, August 22, 1984; J. Maurice LeClair to W. A. Drexel, November 9, 1989 (PF 116); CNGTBN, Coordinated Train Service, March 1996; GTC, Annual Report, 1987, 17; *BN News*, Spring 1989, 16–17; *Wall Street Journal*, December 20, 1989.

23. GTC, Annual Report, 1980, 3; GTW, Minute Book No. 9, 434–435.

24. GTC, Annual Report, 1980, 2; GTC, Five Year Statistical Supplement, 1980–1984; Frank Malone, "GTW-DT&I: A Slow Transition to Avoid Merger Shock," *Railway Age* 181 (June 30, 1981), 38–42; GTC, Annual Report, 1983, 4.

25. GTC, Annual Report, 1981, 6; *GTC Reporter*, August 1986, 2; *Railway Age* 183 (August 30, 1982), 4; GTC, Annual Report, 1984, 8.

26. GTC, Annual Report, 1981, 6; Robert A. Walker to John H. Burdakin, August 11, 1983 (PF 301); GTC, Annual Report, 1985, 16.

27. *Railway Age* 186 (June 1985), 59–60; 186 (October 1985), 26.

28. *GT Reporter*, March 1980, 1; GTC, Annual Report, 1983, 8; *Railway Age* 186 (January 1985), 36–37; GTC, Annual Report, 1984, 8; *Modern Railroads* 40 (June 1985), 24–25; 40 (September 1985), 74–76.

29. GTW, Minute Book No. 7, 328, 345; GTC, Annual Report, 1988, 14, *GT Reporter*, September–October 1983, 5; GTC, Annual Report, 1975, 7; GTW, Minute Book No. 9, 422–423.

30. GTW, Minute Books No. 8, 365–366, No. 9, 466, 474, 480.

31. GTC, Annual Report, 1973, 25, 1979, 6.

32. John H. Burdakin, speech before the American Railway Engineering Association, Chicago, March 22, 1982; John H. Burdakin, comments at Management Meeting, February 3, 1984.

33. *GT Reporter*, July–August 1973, 1; GTC, Annual Reports, 1981, 6, 1985, 4, 5, 14, 15; *Railway Age* 185 (September 1984), 11.

34. J. H. Burdakin and Paul E. Tatro to Coopers & Lybrand, February 17, 1983 (PF 102.11); GTC, Annual Report, 1982, 2, 14, 20.

35. CN, Analysis of Options for the Central Vermont Railway, 1983; P. A. Quesnel to J. M. LeClair, May 17, 1983 (PF 102.11); GTC, Annual Report, 1983, 5.

36. GTC, Annual Reports, 1980, 14, 1983, 14; *GTC Reporter*, August 1986, 2.

37. GTC, Annual Reports, 1982, 14, 1984, 14; *GT Reporter*, March 1984, 2; *Modern Railroads* 40 (June 1985), 20–21.

38. GTC, Annual Reports, 1983, 14, 1984, 14; *GT Reporter*, March 1985, 2; GTC, Annual Report, 1982, 14.

39. GTC, Annual Report, 1983, 14; *GT Reporter*, May 1984, 3; GTC, Five Year Statistical Supplement, 1980–1984 and 1984–1988.

40. Masse, interview, May 24, 1989; DW&P, Duluth Gateway: Loads Handled by Connections, January 7, 1983; DW&P, General Manager files.

41. DW&P, Corporate Records Book 4, May 23, 1973; GTC, Annual Report, 1979, 12; DW&P, Executive Minute No. 51; DW&P, Pokegema Fact Sheet, 1984; "I-35 and the Great Yard Swap," *Railway Age* 186 (April 1985), 45–46.

42. GTC, Annual Reports, 1974, 11, 1980, 12, 1985, 18.

43. John H. Burdakin to J. M. LeClair, October 19, 1984 (PF 103); tabular data from GTC annual reports.

44. William K. Smith, interview, September 24, 1989; Lawless, interview, August 7, 1989; H. Masse, interview, May 24, 1989; David Thomas, "Tough Enough to Hurt," *Canadian Business* 55 (November 1982), 28–34; Burdakin, interviews, November 4, 1989, February 21, 1991; Earl C. Opperthauser, interview, March 6, 1990.

CHAPTER 9. A GREAT RIDE

1. *Modern Railroads* 40 (June 1985), 24–25; 40 (September 1985), 74–76; Summary Statement of John H. Burdakin before the Surface Transportation Sub-committee, July 26, 1984.

2. Art Fettig to the author, July 24, 2013.

3. John H. Burdakin, interview, July 23, 1994.

4. Burdakin, interview, June 6, 2013.

5. These comments derive from responses to questions submitted to those persons cited.

6. Burdakin, interviews, July 23, 1994, June 5, 2013.

7. *GT Reporter* 20 (December 1985), 1; GTC, Annual Report, 1986, 1.

8. Burdakin, interview, June 5, 2013; John Burdakin, annual Christmas letter of 2012 to the author.

9. John H. Burdakin, comments at GT Retiree Luncheon, Royal Oak, Michigan, September 5, 2013.

Index

B

Baggerly, Larry, 18
Bandeen, Robert, 21–28, 30, 54, 71, 73, 75; and Grand
    Trunk Corporation, 45, 61, 92, 95; John Howard
    Burdakin on, 1, 47. *See also under* Canadian National
Barriger, John, 74
Batory, Ronald L., 75, 95
Brewer, James A., 74, 75, 95
Burdakin, Jean, 1, 2, 8, 9, 73, 95
Burdakin, John Howard: and Automatic Car Identi-
    fication, 5–52; business practices of, 34–40, 44,
    47–52, 78–92; and Chicago, Milwaukee, St. Paul
    & Pacific, 61–72; and Detroit, Toledo & Ironton,
    54–59; devotion to good track, 37–38, 40, 85;
    devotion to safe practice, 13, 42, 88, 91, 93, 94;
    foundation principles of, 12, 14, 15, 18, 25–27,
    93–94, 96; at Grand Trunk Corporation and
    Grand Trunk Western, 21–96; how others saw,
    73–75; Jean Burdakin and, 1, 3, 9; in military, 7,
    8; at Panama Canal, 13, 14; parents' influence on,
    5, 6, 7; at Penn Central, 17–19; at Pennsylvania
    Railroad, 11–17; retirement of, 1–3, 95–96
Burdakin, L. Richard, 5, 6, 9
Burdakin, Martha Gertrude, 5, 6, 9
Burlington Northern, 62, 63, 66, 80, 81, 89

C

Cabble, Veronica, 74, 95
Canadian National, 75, 84, 87, 88, 89, 93; Grand
    Trunk Corporation and, 80; Grand Trunk Western
    and, 21, 22, 24, 61–62; Robert L. Bandeen and,
    29, 33–34, 41
Canadian Pacific, 58, 59, 67
Central Vermont, 21, 24, 30, 31, 41, 43, 77, 87–88
Chessie, 54, 58, 82
Chicago & North Western, 23, 61, 62, 65, 66, 67, 68,
    69, 70, 71, 89, 91
Chicago & Western Indiana, 28
Chicago, Milwaukee, St. Paul & Pacific, 61–71, 89, 91
Chicago, Rock Island & Pacific, 61, 62, 63, 65, 66, 67, 70
Cole, Basil, 52, 54–59, 64, 70, 71
Combe, Gloria, 74, 75, 95
Conrail, 47, 52, 61, 77, 78, 79, 80, 82

Coshocton, Ohio, 11, 93
Cramer, Walter H., 24, 27, 43, 65, 73
CSX, 77, 78, 79, 80
Czarnik, Virginia, 74, 75

D

DeBoer, David, 74, 75
Detroit & Toledo Shore Line, 59
Detroit Athletic Club, 1, 95
Detroit Terminal, 21, 40
Detroit, Toledo & Ironton, 54–59, 82, 83, 85
Dole, Elizabeth, 78, 79
Duluth, Missabe & Iron Range, 91
Duluth, Winnipeg & Pacific, 24, 31, 42, 43, 62, 63,
    88–92; as part of Canadian National, 21, 23, 30;
    and Grand Trunk Corporation, 41, 80

E

Elliott, James L., 36

F

Fettig, Art, 93
Flannery, Robert G., 17
Fontaine, Earl G., 73
Ford, Gerald R., 50–51

G

Gelease, Jimmy, 12, 13
General Motors Corporation, 22, 23, 44, 84, 85
Grand Trunk Corporation, 24, 28–29, 45–46
Grand Trunk Western, 21, 22, 49

H

Hagen, James, 75, 80
Higginbotham, Marc, 75, 95
Hrdlicka, Charles, 75, 95

I

Indiana Harbor Belt, 68
Interstate Commerce Commission, 47, 68, 80

K

Kohl, Hank, 93
Krikau, Jim, 74

L

Langdon, Jervis, 56, 79
Larson, Philip C., 41, 42, 74, 75, 87, 88, 95
Lawless, Ron, 1, 69, 92
LeClair, J. Maurice, 71, 75

M

Maas, Gerald, 1, 85, 95
McGee, John, 11, 12
McKnight, William, 74, 75, 95
McMillan, Norman J., 24–25, 29
McMillan, Thomas R., 69, 70
Minneapolis, Northfield & Southern, 67

N

Nicholas, Howard, 74, 95
Norfolk & Western, 54, 55–59, 70, 82
Norfolk Southern, 77, 78, 79, 80

O

Ogilvie, Richard B., 62, 64, 65, 70, 72
Olsen, Byron D., 67, 71
Opperthauser, Earl C., 92

P

Penn Central, 23, 47, 54, 55
Perlman, Alfred, 17, 19
Piggott, W. Douglas, 21
Prorail, 79

R

Roeper, Park, 14

S

Saunders, Stuart T., 17, 19
Schutz, George, 12
Sharp, Robert A., 55, 59
Shepard, Gene, 74, 75, 90, 95
Smith, William K., 92
Smith, Worthington, 62, 65
Soo Line, 63, 67, 68, 69, 70, 91

T

Tatro, Paul, 64, 87
Tischler, Howard, 74, 75, 95

V

vom Eigen, Robert P., 70, 75

W

Walker, Robert A., 80
Wooden, Donald G., 24, 25, 30, 42, 73